Get FIT!

EAT Right!

Be ACTIVE!

GIRLS' GUIDE TO HEALTH & FITNESS

by Michelle H. Nagler

Get FIT!

EAT Right!

Be ACTIVE!

GIRLS' GUIDE TO HEALTH & FITNESS

by Michelle H. Nagler

WNBA

Scholastic Inc.

New York   Toronto   London   Auckland   Sydney
Mexico City   New Delhi   Hong Kong

ACKNOWLEDGMENTS:

The editors and author would like to thank Jeanne Tang, John Hareas, Joe Amati and the rest of the WNBA and NBA management for their helpful access to information and players; Craig Walker, Ellie Berger and Scholastic for making this book a reality; Salvatore Prevete at Madison Square Garden for his encouraging words and smiling face (from Mutt and Jeff); Anthony Falsone for taking the time to share his knowledge about training methods; and, of course, the women of the WNBA, who have established themselves as superior role models for girls everywhere. The players' words, time and insight made working on this book an absolute delight. They are truly inspiring.

Lisa Tartamella and Gretchen Goldfarb generously offered their seemingly boundless nutrition knowledge. Their willingness to be a part of this project was so very appreciated.

The author would also like to give her heartfelt thanks to Bethany Buck and Erin Soderberg. They are wonderful mentors, talented and diligent editors and great b-ball fans to top it off. This book is as much theirs as it is mine.

To Mom, Dad, David, Daniel, Steven and the rest of my beautiful family and friends: your love and support means the world. You guys rock! - MHN

PHOTO CREDITS
NBA Photos / WNBA Enterprises, LLC
Cover (Jennifer Azzi): Sam Forencich. **Cover (Nikki McCray), 38:** Jennifer Pottheiser. **Cover (Teresa Weatherspoon), 47:** Nathaniel S. Butler. **12, 13:** Barry Gossage. **27:** Garrett Ellwood. **36, 61, 67:** Fernando Medina. **39:** Noren Trotman. **57:** Chuck Solomon. **68:** Ray Amati. **87:** Ron Hoskins. **91:** S. Tenuto.

PHOTO CREDITS: INSERT SECTION
NBA Photos / WNBA Enterprises, LLC
I (top): Norm Perdue. **I (bottom):** Barry Gossage. **II (top):** Mitchell Layton. **II (bottom), VIII (top):** Andrew D. Bernstein. **III (top):** Kent Smith. **III (bottom), VIII (bottom):** Gary Bassing. **IV (top):** Ron Hoskins. **IV (bottom):** Rocky Widner. **V (top):** David Sherman. **V (bottom):** Mitchell Layton. **VI (top):** S. Tenuto. **VI (bottom):** Marc Serota. **VII (top):** Greg Shamus. **VII (bottom):** NBA Photo Archives.

12 11 10 9 8 7 6 5 4 3 2 1   1 2 3 4 5 6 / 0

Printed in the U.S.A.
First Scholastic printing, June 2001
Book Design by Peter Koblish

TABLE OF CONTENTS

INTRODUCTION _____7

FITNESS _____9
    Fitness = Fun _____11
    Exercise is, umm, good for you! _____12
    Exercise for the mind _____13
    Let the games begin! How to start exercising _____14
    Goals that score _____17
    Get pumped! _____ 20
    To join or not to join? _____21
    Team sports vs. solo gigs — mini quiz _____23
    Try out and try again _____25
    A note on sportsmanship _____26
    Stand tall _____27

GETTING SPECIFIC:
Components of Physical Fitness _____31
    Mixing it up _____33
    Flexibility _____35
    Warming up _____36
    Flexibility and fitness _____37
    Lower body stretches _____38
    Upper body stretches _____40
    Endurance _____44
    Strength _____46
    Arm exercises with equipment _____53
    Avoiding injury _____56

TABLE OF CONTENTS

Guidance is golden_____59

Mental toughness_____60

How does she hit that shot? And how can I?!_____64

BE ACTIVE_____65

Active lives_____69

NUTRITION IS BALANCE_____73

The C word_____77

The food pyramid — you've seen it a million
times, but do you pay attention?_____78

Dangers of dieting_____86

Some food essentials . . . Power of protein_____90

Calcium and your bones, perfect together_____92

Vitamins and minerals . . . do what?_____96

The skinny on supplements_____97

Vegging out_____99

PLAYERS WITH FITNESS IN THEIR STRIDE__103

Nikki McCray_____105

Natalie Williams_____107

Jennifer Gillom_____109

CONCLUSION: It's All in Your Head_____111

INTRODUCTION

"Regardless of how young or old you are, fitness and being physically fit is huge. Not only for health reasons, but for your self-esteem and self-confidence." — Sheryl Swoopes

Get fit, eat right, be active. It sounds so simple. One plus one plus one equals three. Three aspects of fitness adding up to one healthy mind and body. But this is not simple math. If you want to achieve total wellness, you have to make certain choices, because all three components require motivation and dedication. Building a healthy lifestyle involves physical exercise, good nutrition and a ready mind that is energized, enthusiastic and open to new opportunities and experiences.

Most of this book focuses on the physical — how to get fit by being active and eating right. But wellness also includes your state of mind. If you're not happy with who you are and where you're at, you're not exactly leading a healthy life. The good thing is that taking care of your body will usually up the happiness factor all by itself. If you make fitness and nutrition fun, you'll not only enjoy it; you'll look good and feel better, too.

Players in the Women's National Basketball Association (WNBA) are amazing examples of beautiful women who are strong, energized and active. They will act as role models throughout this book, giving you their secrets for staying in top shape and eating healthy. (They really know their stuff!) And not only are they superb players on the court, they are pretty great people off as well — involved in many other activities, sports and charities. No doubt you will find their stories inspiring and motivating.

"Lifestyle" is a word you will become familiar with while reading this book. You'll get the most out of nutrition and exercise if you incorporate them into your lifestyle (you got it — everyday stuff). Wellness doesn't mean swimming fifteen laps once a month. It means making everyday choices that lead you to a healthier life. It is so easy and so important to start making these choices early on, so they stay with you for life. The sooner you get your body and mind active, the easier it will be to make healthy choices over time.

Don't get nervous — these choices are not totally life changing. In fact, this book will show you how simple it can be to get in shape — no matter what stage you're at. You will learn how to start a fitness program from the very beginning, or how to enhance your lifestyle if you're already leading a pretty active one.

These choices can be combined into three main wellness categories — physical fitness (exercise), nutrition (the food you eat) and your mental state (having a healthy outlook and being a positive, active person). This book will give you the basic info you need to enhance these components of wellness, proving that healthy choices don't have to be difficult. In fact, getting fit should be nothing but fun. It's easy to incorporate good eating habits and simple fitness programs into *everyday* life. You're already on your way. By picking up this book, you've just made your first healthy decision!

Think you're ready for more? Let's get active!

FITNESS

Fitness = Fun

Rivers of sweat, smelly running shoes, sore muscles . . . Who said fitness isn't fun?! Seriously, getting in shape and staying fit does *not* have to mean pain and exhaustion. In fact, the phrase "no pain, no gain" is totally out-of-date. There are loads of ways you can make fitness fun, if you're willing to take the time to find what works for you.

Why? you ask (good thinking). Because if exercise isn't fun, you're not going to want to do it, then you'll start making excuses, and before you know it (eek!) you're a couch slug. So in order to get and stay fit, you have to find activities that *you* enjoy.

WNBA star Chamique Holdsclaw of the Washington Mystics knows the deal. Her advice for starting an exercise program is simply to find something you like to do that will make a workout fun. She explains, "If I'm gonna do cardio, I'll take my headphones with me so I can listen to some music — something that gains my attention so I'm not focused on the treadmill or bike for thirty minutes."

Finding a distraction, like Chamique does, is a great way to pump up a boring workout. But you can bet that she doesn't need any distraction when she's shooting hoops. That's because she found a sport that she enjoys doing. If you can find an athletic activity or sport that you really get excited about, it will make getting fit so much easier and more worthwhile.

If you're already involved in athletic activities you enjoy and you lead an active, healthy life, you're on your way! If not, there is no better time to step it up than right now! Houston

Comet Sheryl Swoopes believes that a healthy life should start as early as possible. She says it's important to get up and moving, especially as a pre-teen. Sheryl explains, "I'd play flag football with my cousins — even tackle. And basketball, softball and all the kid games — like tag, pit and duck-duck-goose." When she

Sheryl Swoopes has always preferred sports and activity to being cooped up inside. Even as a child, she says, "I was never in the house. My mom wanted me to play with dolls and dishes and stuff, but it wasn't my thing."

was young, Sheryl was always up to something. "Any activity I could find to be outside and running around, I was going to do it." Having a fun, active childhood encouraged Sheryl to make it a lifelong habit — being active was fun for her, and she hasn't stopped yet.

Exercise is, umm, good for you!

So sports and exercise are fun (or, they should be anyway). But they are also great for your health (like you needed to be told that). Exercise — the kind where you get out of breath and sweaty — increases your heart rate and makes your muscles and circulatory system really work. It makes your muscles and bones stronger, and your entire body healthier. You'll be less likely to injure yourself, and less likely to get sick (healthy mind and body, and all that stuff). Intense exercise gets your adrenaline pumping and can release these cool things called *endorphins* into your body, which basically make you happy. You know that rush you sometimes get when you're really happy and can't stop smiling? It's that feeling. Of course, that doesn't happen every time — everyone's had their share of misery after a grueling jog where you got caught in the rain, soaked your shoes, got lost. . . . It's not *always* fun, but exercise does usually make you feel better.

Exercise for the mind

In addition to all the health reasons, being physically active is great for self-esteem and self-confidence. Having a healthy body (like having a healthy mind) gives you something to be proud of. It's empowering to know that your body is capable of doing different things — shooting a perfect layup, running a mile or turning a cartwheel. When you're active, you feel better about yourself. Physically, you look better because you are strengthening your muscles, keeping your body trim and

Washington Mystic Nikki McCray says, "Working out makes you feel good and it makes you look healthy. You have a lot of self-confidence when you know that you look good and feel good."

building strong bones. Mentally, you have the satisfaction of knowing you're keeping your body healthy. You may also be better able to focus and concentrate if your body has had physical release, easing tension in your body and your mind.

Sheryl Swoopes said that when she was growing up, basketball was her release, and a great way to escape when she had a rough day. "Whenever I was frustrated about something, or stressed or tense, I would go to the gym and I would just work out my frustrations on the court. I could take the ball and throw it up against the backboard and not hurt anyone or anything. It was just a great release." Life is rough at times; so why not work out your frustrations in a constructive way — instead of bottling up your anger or punching a pillow (which is never as satisfying as you think it'll be)?

Let the games begin! How to start exercising

As a teen, the healthiest thing you can do for your body is to stay active and exercise. So if you're not already doing it, consider this your wake-up kick-in-the-butt. Many experts think it's best to incorporate exercise into daily life — about thirty to sixty minutes of moderate physical exercise every day, like walking to school or riding your bike. According to the American College of Sports Medicine, if you're not hitting the everyday thing, you should be doing at least twenty minutes or more of aerobic exercise three to five times a week. Aerobic means your heart rate is up and you're breathing harder — like when you're jogging or playing basketball. If you're on an athletic team or have gym class in school every day (where you actually break a sweat!), you're probably meeting this mini-

14

mum suggestion for exercise. But if you're a certified couch potato, you might want to jump-start your exercise program. Don't worry. It's not going to be as ugly as it seems. There are a number of easy ways to incorporate exercise into even the least athletic person's life. A few suggestions for the beginner:

● Put one foot in front of the other: Walk. Instead of getting a ride to your friend's house across the neighborhood, why not walk there? Or try activities that involve walking places — like shopping at the mall, hiking or walking to or from school.

● Step it up — meaning, use the stairs. Next time you're waiting for the elevator, think about taking the stairs. And every other day, try taking them double time to push your muscles.

● Rake in the dough. You can turn exercise into a moneymaking enterprise if you rake leaves, mow lawns or shovel snow. Even baby-sitting can be a great aerobic activity — chasing a toddler will most definitely get your heart rate up!

● Grab a friend. Truth: Exercise is much more fun with a friend. So make a pact with your bud to exercise together a few times a week. Gossip while walking around town, rent a cheesy exercise video together or take a class and learn a new skill (boxing, yoga, belly dancing . . . there's so much cool stuff out there).

Washington Mystic Nikki McCray offers some great advice about getting into a new exercise plan. "It's gotta be something you want to do. You can't let people pressure you

Against the Odds

Debbie Black of the Miami Sol is known as "The Pest." In 1997 she was named the American Basketball League's defensive player of the year. When she played for the WNBA's Utah Starzz in 1999, she led the team in steals (77). Debbie is one tough defensive player. Debbie is also five-foot-two — the shortest player in the league. But Debbie doesn't see that as a problem. Instead, she says, "I use [my height] to my advantage because when the ball hits the floor, I'm the closest to it." Debbie stays in top shape by doing a lot of aerobic activity. She tries to be the fittest player in the league, so she can stay at the height of her game.

Despite the way society sometimes acts, your body type *does not* decide your future. Short girls can play basketball. Tall girls can be gymnasts. Beauty queens aren't the only ones in Hollywood. A healthy attitude, determination and some talent will get you far, as long as you believe.

into getting in shape. And then, start small. Start small, and start with a lot of fun stuff you enjoy." Nikki's right — it's tough jumping right into an exercise program cold. You want to ease your body into it, not only to give your muscles time to adjust, but also to get yourself mentally prepared.

If you're just beginning an exercise program, it's important to start slowly so you don't injure yourself or try moves that your body isn't prepared for. How do you make sure you're not moving too quickly? Start with shorter workouts at a lower intensity and gradually step it up. Make sure you're always exercising at a level you feel comfortable with.

You should also try to work exercise into everyday life. Start with a walk around the block, or help carry groceries from the car to the house. You really don't have to jump on a treadmill to start getting in shape. Smaller choices that get your body moving and work your muscles are great. Even if you find you get tired really easily, keep working at it — as you walk a little more every day, you'll build up endurance. The more you carry the groceries, the easier it will be to lift the heavier bags. Try not to be scared or intimidated by fitness — every little choice you make to be more active will help make exercise easier. If you can only do a few sit-ups, keep working on them every night, and pretty soon you'll be able to do lots more.

Getting people to support you is a big help when starting an exercise program. Maybe you can find a friend to work out with you once a week. Or if your mom knows that you want to start exercising, maybe she'll join you in a walk around the neighborhood after dinner. Telling close friends or family about your goals will help motivate you to stick with them.

If you're a fitness rookie, try to avoid becoming insta-exercise girl — you don't want to burn out too quickly because you started working out 24-7. Don't let exercise be a fad, or something you get sick of by overloading in the first two weeks. If you start at an extreme pace or level, you're likely to get bored and tired out quickly. Take your time, and enjoy the strides your body will make — set short- and long-term goals for yourself, so you will have milestones to celebrate your progress.

Goals that score

Goals are important in exercise, the same way they're important in just about any program or long-term project. Setting goals will help you measure your progress and motivate you to stick with it. So it's worth it to really think through your goals and make them obtainable. Make sure you set some

Team Goals

Goals are also important for teams and athletes, since they are often the driving force behind success. Take the Cleveland Rockers, for example. In the 2000 season, they made a team goal. Despite a weak 1999 season, Coach Dan Hughes explained, "Our goal when we met the very first time was to put ourselves in the playoffs." Coach Hughes was confident in his team, and the team had a winning attitude that propelled them through a glorious season. In the middle of the season, Hughes and former Rockers star Suzie McConnell-Serio talked about the things the team had to do in order to reach their goal. Hughes wanted to strengthen their defense, build more depth as a team and gain experience dealing with success and loss. McConnell-Serio talked about building team chemistry that reflected winning attitudes. Working on each of these components is what ultimately helped the Rockers succeed. By focusing on a number of smaller goals, the team reached its overall goal of making the playoffs.

goals that are a bit of a stretch — just mix them in with other short-term goals that you can reach more quickly. Exercise goals should be reasonable and healthy. In other words, don't kid yourself into thinking you will be shooting a perfect hook shot just one month after taking up basketball. It takes time, practice and dedication to perfect shooting skills. A better goal might be to learn five different shots in that month and to be able to sink at least one of each every day.

It's usually best to stay away from goals that are appearance-related. Sure, you want to look as healthy and in-shape as possible. But you're probably not going to get a perfectly flat stomach from playing tennis twice a week. (Washboard abs take a lot of work — and for many people, they're an impossibility!) Instead of focusing solely on looking better, think about how healthy and strong your legs are becoming, how much longer you can rally without tiring or how strong your serve has become. Appearance goals are risky, because everyone is born with a certain body type, and there's only so much you can do to change it. But exercise will build up your endurance, strengthen your heart and tone your muscles. Just one month into starting a fitness program, you'll already be less tired and able to work at a greater intensity.

Women's bodies are all different — curvy, thin, broad, petite, muscular. It's important to take pride in whatever your body type, in order to think positively about yourself. Exercising will keep your body fit and active and totally up your self-esteem. It can also take off a few extra pounds and tone up your muscles. But exercising to change your whole body type will usually cause you hurt — physically and mentally. If you're trying to change something beyond your control, you can cause yourself injury (not to mention a ton of frustration). If you find that your exercise goals are all about your butt or your waistline, even though you try to focus your mind elsewhere, you might want to try talking to a fitness professional, school nurse or doctor.

Getting in shape is about making small life changes over time and adopting a healthy attitude toward exercise and nutrition. Fitness is not about starving and sweating your way to insta-model status. (Reality check: Most of us will not emerge from the gym as supermodels.) Wellness is *overall* body health — where you look and feel strong and healthy.

The best exercise goals are those that push your body just enough so you are constantly reaching new levels and making new goals to increase your physical activity. You want to

Reward Yourself

When you reach your goals, don't forget to reward yourself!! Here are ten suggestions to get you started:

1. Soak in a warm tub with yummy smelling bath oil.

2. Ice cream! C'mon, everyone deserves it.

3. Veg out in front of the TV with a favorite show . . . and pretend you lost the remote.

4. Buy that lip gloss / book / CD you've been eyeing at the mall.

5. Get some beauty rest — play soothing music, put your feet up, maybe even cover your eyes with cucumber slices.

6. Give yourself a manicure or pedicure — or better yet, trade them with a friend.

7. Bake cookies and invite friends over to share.

8. Listen to your favorite song — over and over again.

9. Make yourself a fruit smoothie. They're delicious and healthy! (Check out a great recipe on page 77)

10. Find a quiet corner, get comfy and lose yourself in a good book.

maintain a healthy level of fitness — neither slack too much, nor push yourself so hard that you risk injury. It is certainly possible to work out too much, and be too obsessive about it.

Get pumped!

You know that exercise is supposed to be fun, but sometimes you're just not in the mood. What can you do to get yourself psyched up? Some WNBA players have pregame rituals or workout traditions that get them pumped. Try one on the next time you're feeling low:

◯ Chamique Holdsclaw listens to music when she works out. Her top choices? DMX and Jay Z.

◯ The Indiana Fever's Kara Wolters also uses music to get herself psyched — Van Halen is a favorite. Kara also insists on showering before every game, even though she's just going to go out there and sweat like crazy!

● Vicky Bullett of the Washington Mystics likes to keep her head clear until right before tipoff. She wants to stay mentally focused and not stress herself out before a game. In case any bad thoughts sneak in during warm-ups, she knocks on the floor right after the national anthem to chase them away.

● Dawn Staley of the Charlotte Sting likes to soak in a cold Jacuzzi to get her muscles pumped.

● Pregame, New York Liberty star Becky Hammon . . . sleeps. Go figure! She likes to be well rested for the game so she can give it her all.

To join or not to join?

There are two main ways to get involved in athletics — you can join a team or club, or do it on your own. In other words, you can try "organized sports" (like joining a b-ball team) or stick to more informal, on-your-own workouts (like playing pick-up hoops in the park). Both will get you totally fit, and are great for your health.

If you're more the informal type and don't like participating in organized sports, that's okay. There are still tons of ways you can be athletic and stay in shape, and lots of reasons why you might want to get fit on your own terms. Maybe you like having the freedom to be creative with your workouts — you don't want anyone telling you what exercises to do and when to do them. Or perhaps exercise is your "me" time, when you get in touch with your thoughts and sort through the day. Maybe it's a time thing — you want to run for however long *you* want to run and at times that are good for you. (This is especially common for girls who are busy with other non-athletic activities.) Or maybe varying your workout is how you keep motivated — one day boxing, the next ballet. This is great. Working out with a friend is another great way for the independent athlete to get motivated without joining the structure of a team or class. As long as you're staying active, working out on your own outside of a team, club, or class is totally fine.

If you participate in organized sports (like playing softball in a local league, or joining your school's football team), it may be easier to stay motivated. For one, team sports tend to be more structured, so it's harder to use the "I'm tired today" excuse. If exercise is penned into your days, it's easier to get into a routine. If you know you have Tae Kwon Do class every Thursday, you'll look forward to going all week. That feeling of organization can really help get you psyched.

There's also a feeling of togetherness that goes with organized sports, which acts like a big motivator. You get to hang out with other people who enjoy the same thing you do. Taking a class (like ice-skating or karate) can be a great way to meet people — and you already have something to bond about! Look at buddies Teresa Weatherspoon and Nikki McCray — they got totally close because of the game. Or the entire Los Angeles Sparks team — when they want to joke around together, they play a game called "Make Me Laugh," where they try to make each other laugh and the first one to bust out loses (Lisa Leslie says DeLisha Milton is the champ!).

Joining a team is the most common way to get involved in organized sports. Sue Wicks of the New York Liberty supports team sports in a big way. She says, "Women on teams have support when they're working out. They're building relationships with other women; it's great to be competitive and work together toward a goal. But it doesn't only happen on the sports field. They're also getting in shape together and living a good healthy lifestyle." Sue thinks teams act as big support systems — something that can be especially important for pre-teens and teens.

Team sports vs. solo gigs

As any WNBA player will tell you, there are definite advantages to team sports. But that's not to say individual sports aren't totally great, too. Are you a team player? Or more the solo star? Take this mini quiz to see where you might be better suited:

1. **Imagine you've got the voice of Lauryn Hill. You rock! Would you rather:**
   A. Sing with a choir?
   B. Flaunt it in a solo performance?

2. **Your friends are more likely to describe you as:**
   A. Supportive, a good listener.
   B. A talker, often the center of attention.

3. **Big oral report in English class. You'd much rather:**
   A. Work in a group. If everyone does their share, it will turn out a much better project.
   B. Work alone. You don't want to worry about sharing responsibility with anyone who might not do their part.

4. Mom sends you out with a list of groceries. But you can't find that special lettuce she wants. You: .

    A. Ask a store clerk to point you in the right direction.

    B. Search all over the produce department — you like the challenge and will feel good when you find it.

5. School dance! The lights are flashing, the music's blaring and you're dancing up a storm. Are you:

    A. Grooving in a circle of gals?

    B. Bustin' out in the middle of the circle?

Now tally 'em up. Did you have mostly A's or B's?

Mostly A's: Groupie Gal

If you picked **A** most of the time, you may be better suited to team sports. You work well in a group, and you enjoy the support you get from sharing activities with other people. Rock on! Your team spirit is terrific, and people probably love having you on their side! Just be sure to remember how special you are, too. Your contribution to the team or group is just as important as everyone else's — don't be afraid to shine once in a while!

Some sports you might try: basketball, softball, cheerleading, soccer, volleyball, football, field hockey, lacrosse

Mostly B's: Solo Sister

If you picked mostly **B**'s, you may be more into individual sports. You're not afraid of the spotlight, and you like taking responsibility for your own actions. That's a great thing! Just

24

be careful to let others shine, too. And don't be too hard on yourself. The same way it's more difficult to be a gloryhog in team sports, it can be hard to accept defeat when it's just you competing in an individual sport. Realize that your best is all you can ask of yourself!

Some sports you might try: skiing, gymnastics, tennis, track, golf, swimming, fencing, cross country

Added bonus: Lots of solo sports have a team aspect to them, too. These are sports where you compete as an individual, but have the support of a team behind you. If you play one of these sports on a team, you still have the individual attention, but you also have a bunch of team members to celebrate with when you succeed and to support you when you have a bad match or meet.

Try out and try again

What if you try out for a sports team and don't make it? Unfortunately, this is pretty common. First of all, realize that this is not going to be your only opportunity to get involved with athletics, even with that particular sport. There may be other leagues, other sports and there is always next year. To up your chances of making the team in the future, ask the coach what skills you need to improve on, then practice, practice and practice some more! Enlist the help of friends and family to really work on your game. You could also think about helping the team in another way, like keeping score or acting as a trainer. You will learn a lot and impress the coach. Lastly, don't even think about ditching the games! Showing your support as a fan will show

Variety Is the Spice of Life

WNBA players are total b-ball freaks, of course. But did you know that the players are active in sports and fitness in lots of ways outside of basketball? Many vary their workouts with running, cycling or swimming. And most WNBA stars have other sports they play for fun on the side. Ruthie Bolton-Holifield of the Sacramento Monarchs likes to play tennis. So does the Phoenix Mercury's Michele Timms. Sheryl Swoopes keeps the ball in the air playing volleyball for fun. And Washington Mystic Vicky Bullett is awesome at softball! Part of being an athlete is having overall athletic ability — not just being super good at one sport or skill.

the team and coaches that you're dedicated, and it will teach you more about strategy, the other players and the coach's style.

A note on sportsmanship

Being a team player means displaying good sportsmanship. If you've ever been on a team before, no doubt your coach explained this a hundred times. Sportsmanship is a big part of being physically fit and being an athlete, because the athletic community is just that — a community. Sports have rules and etiquette, just like school, youth groups and social situations. If you want to be an active, successful athlete, you have to follow those rules — play fair, show a positive attitude, don't treat your opponents in an unfair or unsportsmanlike way, etc. You know the drill. Being a good sport is also a way of showing that you're mentally in the game, and that you have the right attitude about yourself and your fellow players.

Dawn Staley of the Charlotte Sting was the WNBA's recipient of the Sportsmanship Award in 1999. The award is based on a player's commitment to the spirit of sportsmanship and ethical play. Dawn was selected because of her honorable behavior on the court as well as her remarkable contributions to society off the court. She runs her own foundation that organizes a number of community projects for inner-city kids and

A good sport and a natural leader! Dawn Staley was selected as a co-captain for Team USA at the 2000 Olympic Games in Sydney. She led her team to a golden victory!

young adults, including after-school projects, a basketball league and special events.

Stand tall

Six-foot-five Houston Comet Monica Lamb was six-foot-four when she was just twelve years old. She says, "I was just lucky that I had older sisters who wouldn't let me feel bad about being tall. They would pinch me in the back of my neck and say, 'Sit up straight. Sit up straight. You have to sit up straight.' And so because of that, it's become a habit for me to practice good posture."

You may not tower over the six-foot mark like Monica, but her sisters' age-old advice still applies to every woman no matter what her height. Stand. Up. Straight. It's especially important to develop good posture at a young age, because if you're not keeping your spine in line now, it'll be much harder to get in the habit later in life.

If you slouch a lot or hunch over when you stand, you're not giving your muscles a chance to work properly. You're taking the easy way out and, as a result, you're weakening your back, stomach and leg muscles. The more you slump, the more your muscles get used to being in that position. And that weakening can cause major problems later in life. Bad posture is also a problem right now. People who slouch appear less confident and less in shape. That's right — standing up straight instantly improves your appearance by making you look leaner, healthier and more graceful.

Take it from six-foot-five Lisa Leslie of the Los Angeles Sparks, whose mother encouraged her to be proud of her height. Of course, being tall has helped Lisa's game, but she has also said that without her mother's encouragement, "I don't think I would have been able to stick with it and been proud of who I am and be feminine on the court. I think I would have folded to the peer pressure if I didn't have my mom to encourage me to be proud of how tall I am." Lisa's mom knew it was important for her daughter to be proud of herself — whatever her height. And that's true for every girl. No matter what your height or body type, standing tall and being proud is the healthy choice.

What can you do to improve your posture? That's the best part: Standing tall is possibly the easiest way you can improve your health (and appearance!). It really is this simple: Stand up straight. To make sure you've got it right, take a look in the mirror to see if your body is lining up correctly. Your head should be held up so your ears are in line with your shoulders, your shoulders should fall into line over your hips, your hips are lined up over your knees, and your knees above your feet.

Making a conscious effort to walk with your head up can make a big difference. If you want to really work at getting good posture, stretching and strength training will do wonders. Six-foot-two Rushia Brown of the Cleveland Rockers is a big fan of stretching to help her posture (and her game): "I have a history of back problems so I do a lot of extra back stretching, trying to get flexibility since I'm really stiff."

One of the most effective back stretches is also an exercise in posture, and can be done just about anywhere. Reach forward and try to touch your toes, letting your head hang loose and making sure not to lock your knees. Slowly roll up to standing, taking your time to breathe deeply and concentrate on stacking your vertebrae directly on top of one another in a straight line. Your head should be the last thing to come up, balancing itself directly on top of your (now straight) spine.

Strength training also helps posture because it allows you to strengthen the muscles that keep your body in line. The muscle groups that support your back — abs (stomach muscles), glutes (butt muscles) and hamstrings (the muscles in the backs of your thighs) — are all important muscles to strengthen.

Stretching and lifting weights are great for your back, assuming you don't overdo it. But take notice — standing and sitting up straight automatically works these muscle groups for you, too. In other words, good posture breeds good posture.

No matter what your height, good posture is a great way

to improve your health and overall appearance. Not only does it strengthen your muscles, it makes you look and feel better. Standing tall is all good, and nothing bad. So HEY YOU! What are you doing slouching over reading this book? Sit up straight, relax your shoulders and lift that chin. You got it girl! Way to stand tall.

GETTING SPECIFIC:
Components of Physical Fitness

Mixing it up

There are three important parts of physical fitness: flexibility, endurance and strength. Each of these pieces improves your body in a different way, but all three are linked. It is important to develop and maintain all three components of fitness equally to keep your body balanced. If you neglect one, you may become more prone to injury and find it harder to get in shape. As an athlete, that means your body won't be as capable of performing at its most competitive level. As a generally healthy person, if you're not in balance physically, you're making it harder for yourself to stay healthy and fit.

For example, some girls think that in order to get "in shape" all they need to do is hours and hours of cardiovascular exercise. They want to lose weight, but not "bulk up," so they ignore strength training altogether. Sound familiar? If so, you are doing your body a disservice by leaving out some components of a balanced workout. If you ignore strength training, you're building less muscle. After a certain amount of cardio exercise, you will have built up endurance, but your muscles may be lacking. Without stronger, more powerful muscles, you are limiting your athletic performance. You are also (listen up — this might surprise you) not getting any skinnier. If your goal in doing nothing but cardio is to slim down, you're cheating yourself. Adding in some strength training will tone your muscles and increase your metabolism — meaning you'll look better *and* burn more fat.

Mixing it up doesn't just mean working each of the different components — strength, endurance and flexibility. You also want to work different muscle groups as you go, to develop all of your body in a variety ways. For example, if you do arm-strengthening exercises with three-pound weights every night, you need to balance that by working your lower body, too. It's important to work your entire body — not just, say, your abs, because you want a smaller waistline. Think of your body as one unit where every muscle is working together, and every part relies on another.

Mixing it up also means trying different activities to keep yourself interested. (A bored athlete is not going anywhere!) If you hate swimming, but force yourself to swim laps every day, you're going to burn out quickly and start hating the idea of exercise. That's not the goal. You'd be better off combining swimming with other activities, like walking your dog or Rollerblading, or cut out the swimming altogether and focus on a sport you do enjoy.

Trying new sports and activities builds different skills, which makes you well rounded. Many sports rely on one another and borrow from one another. For example, many divers have gymnastics backgrounds, and lots of soccer players also play lacrosse or run track. WNBA star Natalie Williams, for example, likes doing deep-water conditioning exercises for endurance and strength, and yoga for strength, flexibility and mental focus. Both of these workouts help Natalie's basketball game!

To mix up your workouts, keep them different and work different parts of your body. And most of all, make sure they include all three elements of fitness — flexibility, endurance and strength. In order for you to learn to really work all three areas of fitness into the workout you create, this section will explain each area separately.

Flexibility

Some people are born with the ability to touch their toes. For others, it can be a lifelong pursuit. Flexibility might come easier to some, but anyone can work on and develop better flexibility. And it can be one of the most enjoyable, relaxing and rewarding elements of a workout if you take your time and do it correctly.

To increase flexibility, all you have to do is stretch. Take a few minutes before and after every workout to stretch out those tight muscles. Sounds pretty simple, right? It is. So why do people continually ignore stretching and not give it the credit it deserves? Often it's because of time — you want to get started so you can finish your workout sooner. But this is just not smart.

Pre-practice or pregame stretches get your muscles primed to work out and decrease your chance of injury. They are the most common type of stretches. If you've ever played on any kind of team, no doubt your coach did at least some kind of pre-workout stretching. It's pretty important. Remember though: it's best to stretch after a warm-up. The next section will go into more in-depth info about the all-important (and often ignored) first step of a workout: the warm-up.

But don't just stretch before your workout. Also be sure you take time to cool down and stretch your muscles after you exercise, so they don't stay tight or get knotted. When you work out, blood pumps through your muscles, sometimes causing a buildup of certain products, like lactic acid, which can cause your muscles to cramp (ouch!). Cool downs and post-practice stretching clean out your muscles, helping them to recover quicker.   A good cool down will include not only a few minutes of slower movement to gradually slow your heart rate, it will also include stretching. As far as flexibility is concerned, there is no better time to work on it than after your workout, when your muscles are already warm.

Warming up

The purpose of the warm-up (which comes *before* stretching!) is simple enough — to raise your body temperature. But along with that, it warms your muscles, gets blood flowing through them and lubricates joints — priming your body to be stretched and exercised.

A warm-up only needs to take about three to five minutes. A good rule of thumb is to slowly go over every move you will do during your workout. For example, if you're about to play volleyball, warm up with the motions you'll use in the game: bending your knees and moving low to the ground, jumping as if you were spiking an imaginary ball, and swinging your arms as if to serve. When in doubt, a few minutes of jogging or jumping jacks will always work as a general full-body warm-up Once your muscles are warm, they are ready to be stretched.

The Cleveland Rockers warm up together with fun, active stretches. High kicks stretch your legs and get your heart pumping!

The Indiana Fever makes warming up an important part of their routine. Before every practice, the team does active stretches together to get their bodies moving. Instead of concentrating only on static stretches, where you stretch your muscles in place, they incorporate stretching into their warm-up by doing leg swings and modified jogging with butt kicks and high knees.

Flexibility and fitness

In addition to protecting you from injury, stretching can make your workout more worthwhile. For one thing, flexibility may improve the effects of strength training. If you focus on strength but ignore flexibility, your muscles (the ones you've worked so hard to strengthen) will suffer. You limit your muscles' range of motion, and stop them from working at maximum capacity. No matter how strong you try to make your muscles, if they are not able to bend, move and stretch they are much more likely to get strained or torn. Some experts think that stretching your muscles during strength training may actually increase the effects of the strength workout.

Ideally, you should stretch your whole body if you want to increase flexibility. But if this isn't going to happen, you should at least stretch the muscles you'll utilize in your workout. If you're running, for example, you want to make sure to concentrate on stretching your lower body (legs, glutes, lower back). Of course, it would be awesome if you have the time to stretch your upper back, arms and chest, too.

Vicky Bullett has made stretching a regular part of her life, as well as her workout. "Stretching is always the best way to start the day," she says. "Even if you're not an athlete, you should stretch. It keeps your muscles warm, it gets you

"I really take a lot of pride in stretching," Vicky Bullett says. She is careful to take her time and make sure all her muscles are warmed up before she starts her workout.

going. And if you are an athlete, it's so important to warm up those muscles before you start working out."

Lower body stretches

Quadriceps and calf stretches: These are pretty common stretches — and they're easy to do standing up. For the quad stretch, stand up, bend one leg and hold your foot behind you, pulling it toward your butt. You want to be careful to keep your leg in line (don't bring your foot to the side of your body), or you'll put stress on your knee.

Stretching your calves is also pretty simple — all you need is a wall. Stand facing the wall with one foot in front of the other, a few feet apart, hands in front of you on the wall. In this lunge position, you want to push against the wall while straightening your back leg. You should feel the stretch in your back calf; if you don't, simply move your leg farther back. Note: This is also a good position from which to stretch your Achilles tendon (the tendon that runs along the back of your ankle). Hurting this tendon results in a serious, painful injury, so it's a good idea to stretch your Achilles often (particularly if you wear high- or chunky-heeled shoes). While in the calf stretch, just bend your back knee to stretch your Achilles.

Hamstrings, hips and butt stretches: You can stretch your hamstrings by sitting on the ground, legs straight out in front of you. Bend one leg in so the sole of your foot is touching your inner thigh. Bend forward and reach for the out-stretched foot, feeling the stretch in your hamstring. Switch sides to stretch the other leg. Some people find it easier to isolate the hamstring if you lie on your back and pull one leg toward you — using your hands or even a towel.

The outer thigh muscle that surrounds your hip is called the abductor. You can stretch the abductor by sitting on the floor with your legs straight out in front of you. Take one leg, cross it over the other and hug your knee to your chest. Feel that pulling in your bent leg's hip? That's your abductor. Another way to stretch your abductor is by sitting in a butterfly position but with your feet further out in front of you, forming an elongated diamond shape. Stretch forward and try to touch your nose to your feet. You should feel the stretch in your butt and hips.

Pregame, Sue Wicks stretches her outer thigh (abductor) and butt muscles (glutes). With all the running Sue does on the court, this is an important stretch!

"A Player's Perspective"

Chamique Holdsclaw loves stretching her hamstrings, and she tries to do it as often as she can — before, after, even during her workouts. She says she likes that stretch because, "I'm not very flexible, and I know that two of the most important things for me are my hamstrings and hip flexors." Having flexibility in hamstrings and hip flexors is important to all athletes. Basketball players, especially, spend so much time sprinting and jumping that they usually have a great amount of strength in their legs and work those muscles hard in each game or practice.

Your adductor muscle is your inner thigh, which you can stretch in a straddle position — legs bent in a butterfly or outstretched. Just bend forward, keeping your back straight and try to touch your nose to the ground.

You StairMastered — and now your butt's killing you. Here's the stretch to know: Lie flat on the floor with your knees bent (sit-up position). Take one leg and bend it, resting that ankle on your other thigh. Reach behind that thigh and gently pull it toward you, keeping your opposite foot balanced on the thigh. You should feel the stretch in your butt (your *gluteus maximus*, of course), and on the side of the top leg.

Upper body stretches

Girls tend to forget about upper body stretches (admit it — we do!), because many of our workouts focus on leg activities, like running, stepping or bicycling. But the upper body *is* an important area to work on and stretch. Even if you're just doing cardio (not a good thing — but let's move on), the exercise will almost always involve arm motion, and it will certainly work stomach and back muscles.

Arm stretches are pretty straightforward — basically, move your arm until you feel a stretch. To break it down, though, let's start with your **triceps**. Extend one arm above your head. Bend it at the elbow so that you're reaching down your back. With your opposite arm, gently push your elbow back behind your head. You should feel the stretch in the underside of your upper arm (your triceps).

If you're a volleyball or tennis player, you know the value of the **forearm stretch**. To stretch your forearm (the inner side of your lower arm), straighten your arm out in front, palm facing up. With the other hand, grasp your fingers and gently pull them back toward your body. You might not feel this stretch as strongly as others, but that doesn't mean it isn't working!

Shoulder stretch: Your shoulders can be stretched in a number of ways. One method is to clasp your hands behind your lower back, arms straight, palms facing your back. Gently raise your arms up, keeping them clasped. It is also helpful to have a friend raise your arms in this position for a better stretch. Another way to stretch your shoulders is by reaching one arm straight across the front of your body, at about chest level. Grasp it with your other hand or in the crook of your other arm, pulling it toward you. You should feel the stretch as you pull your arm toward you. Finally, stretch the top of your shoulders (closer to your neck) and upper back, by reaching your arms straight out in front of you and clasping your hands together. Push out and exhale.

Lower back: The "T" Stretch is a great way to stretch

Yoga

Yoga is all over the place today — in magazines, at the gym, even in the WNBA. Natalie Williams, for one, is a huge yoga fan. She believes yoga is a great way to increase flexibility, self-control and to relax her body. Difficult? Yes. Rewarding? Absolutely.

Yoga (which means "union" in Sanskrit) was developed in India as a spiritual exercise that allowed individuals to get in touch with themselves as well as with spirituality. Today, it's more commonly used in America as a form of exercise and relaxation. Yoga is said to reduce tension, improve circulation, and increase flexibility, muscle tone and strength.

When trying out yoga positions, it is especially important to go slowly and not push yourself. Many yoga positions require an incredible amount of flexibility, concentration and balance. Don't hurt yourself trying a skill you're not yet capable of doing. Also don't get frustrated — with practice, you'll be able to work up to the more difficult moves. It is also important in yoga to have a guide. A personal instructor is best, but if you don't have access, pay close attention to instructional books and videos. Form is extremely important.

Two basic moves in yoga are the dog and the cat, which increase flexibility in the spine. To try these moves, get down on your hands and knees, with your knees about hip width apart, and your hands slightly in front of your shoulders, fingertips pointing forward. Point your toes (don't curl them up). Start by inhaling and arching your back downward — push your stomach and chest to the floor as you tilt your pelvis up and lift your head. Feel the gentle stretch in your spine and stomach? This position is the dog. As you exhale, you're going to flow into the cat position by bringing in your chest and stomach, and curving your spine upward. Your back should round up, while your pelvis tilts downward. Let your head drop, easing the tension in your neck. Repeat this sequence several times, moving smoothly from dog to cat and back to dog. Concentrate on your breathing and gentle stretches.

your lower back — and it feels great. Lie on the floor, faceup, with your arms outstretched (hence the "T" position). Take one leg and cross it over your body, trying to keep your back and arms on the floor. If you don't feel the stretch, try turning your head to face away from your crossed leg. Go back to starting position and try it in the other direction.

Stomach: Abdominal muscles are a tough set to stretch. If you're extremely flexible (or a gymnast), you can do a bridge, which works wonders. But most people struggle with this flexibility exercise. If you have access to a large blow-up exercise ball, you can roll back on it, arching over it until you feel a stretch. Basically the motion is the same as in a bridge — you're arching your back and elongating your stomach muscles. Perhaps the simplest method of stretching your abs is a yoga pose called the dog, which is explained at left.

Your oblique muscles are found on the sides of your stomach. To stretch these, you can obviously bend sideways, but another effective stretch is this: sit on the floor, legs out in front of you. Bend one leg and rest that foot on the inner thigh of the outstretched leg. Placing your opposite hand on the bent leg knee, twist your torso toward the bent leg. Switch legs and twist toward the other side.

Easy ways to increase flexibility:

- Stretch your muscles before and after every workout.
- Make stretching a part of your everyday life by stretching out when you wake up or before you go to bed.
- Try stretching when you're gabbing away on the phone or while watching TV. Give some purpose to a usually non-fitness activity.
- Go slowly and concentrate on your breathing while stretching. Make sure you're taking long, full breaths both in and out.

Endurance

You sweat, your heart is pumping, your feet barely touch the ground. If you're not flirting with the homeroom hottie, you're probably doing cardio exercise. Cardiovascular exercise is an endurance workout. It works your cardiovascular system — your heart and blood vessels. Your heart is a muscle, which (as you probably know) pumps blood through the body. When you do aerobic exercise and increase your heart rate, what you are actually doing is working the heart muscle and pumping blood quicker. It's like strength training for the heart.

As you practice cardio exercise, you increase your endurance. Your heart becomes stronger, gaining the ability to pump more blood through your body. It also learns to use oxygen more efficiently, which allows you to exercise for longer periods of time and at greater levels of intensity. Cardiovascular exercise makes for a healthier body. Done regularly, it can decrease your chance of heart disease (the number-one cause of death in America), and may prevent certain cancers and illnesses. Cardio exercise will also give you more energy, help you lose excess body fat and increase flexibility and range of motion.

How do you know what counts as cardiovascular activity? Basically, if your heart rate is up, you're doing it. It should be aerobic — which means that you're breathing hard and taking in a lot of oxygen. You should do the exercise (which is usually rhythmic and repeated) for an extended period of time — ideally, for at least twenty minutes. Some classic examples of cardio activity are jogging, jumping rope, swimming and cycling. But there are lots of different exercises that can fall under the cardio territory — for example, rock climbing, kick-

Water, Water, Everywhere . . .

Staying hydrated while you're working out is extremely important. When you exercise, your body temperature rises and you sweat (unless you're too perfect to sweat, in which case you should shut this book right now). When your body heats up, it uses water to cool itself — by sweating. It's a neat system, really. The only downside is that you're losing water. So it's important to stay hydrated, replacing the water you lose during exercise. Because the cells in your body need water to perform properly, if you're dehydrated you aren't performing at your best level, and your heart has to work that much harder to compensate. You might feel unusually tired, get a headache or even pass out. And if you're exercising in the sun, WELL! Your body's using even more water, so double the advice — drink more!

In general, drinking water is a bonus because it's great for your skin and for general health, even when you're not working out. Water carries nutrients through your body, refreshing and cleaning out your system. Natalie Williams knows how important water is to her performance. Her teammates tease her constantly about her water because she can't leave home without it! She says that water affects every part of her body — and she's right.

You feel thirsty, you drink. Right? Sorry, try again. Using thirst as an indication that you need to drink more water is not a good game plan. Thirst is a sign of dehydration, meaning that once you're thirsty, you're already dehydrated. It's too late. Your plan of attack needs to be to drink water *before* you get thirsty.

So what if you hate drinking water? Kara Wolters offers a tip: Put lemon in it to add flavor. You can also try orange slices, fresh mint sprigs, even some of the fruity powdered stuff (though beware of high sugar contents!).

boxing, dancing, blading, kayaking and hiking.

WNBA teams do tons of cardio, especially at the beginning of the season, to build endurance. Players need to stay strong on the court for long periods of time, while playing at a high-intensity level. Lots of teams do shooting and running drills, which allow them to increase their endurance while tuning up b-ball skills.

Though moderate exercise is ideal to greatly improve your

cardiovascular system, you should do more than just exercise for extended periods of time. You should make smaller lifestyle adjustments that will also benefit your heart and endurance (see the box below for more info).

Easy ways to increase endurance:

- Walk the dog (no pet? Borrow a neighbor's — they'll be psyched!)
- Pair up with a friend to hike or walk around town
- Take the stairs
- Walk or bike to school
- Grab headphones and window-shop through the mall at turbo speed
- When forced to clean your room, turn up the music and dance, jump and spin yourself into a cleaning (and calorie-burning) whirlwind

---

Strength

Strength training. The very words sound awesome and powerful. Strength training. It's hardcore and tough and all those cool things. But there's one thing that strength training shouldn't be: intimidating. Strong is good. Powerful is feminine. Strength training is (dare I say it?) fun.

Nykesha Sales is one of the WNBA's powerhouses of strength. She is a turbo-woman in the weight room, but she's also well aware of the importance of keeping her routine balanced. She says, "Strength is my strong suit. I am not as flexible as I would like to be. As an athlete, this is an area where a

lot of injures can result, so my
flexibility is something that I am
always working on. Endurance
is another area that I work to
improve on. But I *am* strong."

When you strength train,
you are not just building stronger
muscles (though that *is* the main
goal). You're also building a
stronger body. Strength training

Nykesha Sales is totally fit and strong. What's her
secret? Her advice is, "Find something you love doing, so
that you want to do it every day. Exercise doesn't have
to be a chore!"

affects bones, tendons, your heart and lungs — just about every
part of your body. Done correctly, strength training can be one of
the most rewarding parts of your workout, because it's possible
to see results pretty quickly.

You know that strength training toughens your muscles.
But did you know it increases bone density? After a few
months of strengthening your muscles, mysterious things
called muscle myoproteins, bone osteoproteins and minerals
all increase in your body — and they help make your bones
stronger.

Increasing muscle mass can also increase your metabolism. Sound strange? It's actually quite logical. Your body has
to burn more calories to maintain muscle. So even when
you're not working out, your body will burn more calories just
by having extra muscle to care for. To put this in real figures,

every pound of muscle on your body burns up to fifty calories a day — just by existing! Be aware that muscle weighs more than fat, though, so even if you feel yourself getting stronger and can see your body toning up, you might actually be gaining weight.

Lifting weights is not the only way to strength train, but it is probably the most common method. Unfortunately, there is a major stereotype (ahem, MYTH!) about weight lifting that many people believe. *Lifting weights will cause you to bulk up.* Don't believe the hype! Most athletic trainers and strength coaches will tell you that it is pretty difficult for a woman to put on a lot of muscle mass and bulk up. We would have to consume *a lot* of calories (more than the norm), exercise about five or more times a week, and possibly take nutritional supplements, too. Of course, the likelihood of bulking up depends largely on genetics, too, but in general, it's not going to happen just by investing in a set of dumbbells. Lifting weights is often a major component of strength training — and it's an extremely valuable and underrated part of a total body workout. So don't skip it because you think you'll get huge. You won't.

You may have heard that lifting weights can be harmful if you start too young. For example, that it can stunt your growth or cause injury. This is not completely false. It *is* possible to cause damage to your bones if you lift too much, particularly at a young age when your bones are still growing. During adolescence, it's safest to stick to lighter weights and avoid heavy power lifting. If you can do fifteen reps comfortably, you are probably working at an acceptable level. It's also a good idea to use your own body weight for resistance, like with push-ups and pull-ups. And if you have any concerns about strength training, talk to a strength coach or fitness specialist who can better evaluate what level your body is capable of working at.

To start a strength-training program, there are three basic concepts you need to get: *recovery*, *balance* and *adaptation*. More specifically, when you start lifting, you'll want to structure your workout into *sets* and *reps*. Here's the skinny:

Recovery is exactly what it sounds like — the amount of time your muscles need to recover. You don't want to work the same muscle two days in a row. The most common way to solve this is to work different muscle groups every other day. A lot of people find it easiest to remember this rule by working upper body muscles one day and lower body the next. But you can mix it up any way you like.

The second concept is **balance** — every muscle in your body is "balanced" by another. Triceps / biceps, quadriceps / hamstrings, abdominals / back . . . you get the point. The same way it is important to balance your workout between different components of physical fitness, it is also important to balance your strength training between opposing muscle groups. You don't want to overdevelop your triceps without working your biceps. They work together, so make sure you give them both their due.

Adaptation refers to the way that your muscles get used to the work they do — they adjust by getting stronger. That's why it's important to do different exercises to strengthen the same muscles. One great plan is to redesign your workout every few weeks to make sure you're keeping it fresh. Also, talk to fitness trainers and coaches to learn new exercises, and check out fitness magazines and web sites that have special sections for teens.

When you're ready to lift, you'll break your workout into two groups: **reps** and **sets**. A rep is one full motion of a certain exercise — usually, lifting the weight and lowering it back to starting position. A set is the number of reps you do in sequence. For example, you might do three sets of fifteen reps each. (Remember to rest between sets!) To make sure that you are actually increasing strength, the muscle should be exhausted by the end of your last set — no matter how many sets you do, the resistance should be enough so that by the end, you are unable to do any more reps. The number of sets and reps you do depends on your strength training goals and the exercise you are doing. The best way to get a personalized weight-training program is to talk to a coach or weight training specialist.

If you're struggling with strength training, fret not. It takes time and persistence to build muscle power — doing a few arm curls one day won't make you buff overnight. Jennifer Gillom of the Phoenix Mercury can relate. She knew her upper body needed work, so she decided to start doing push-ups. But there was a slight problem — she couldn't even do *one*. She didn't give up, though. Instead, she did one push-up a day and worked her way up from there. Now she can do more than forty! "I'd add on about three to four more every week, and I just gradually built myself up that way."

Jennifer found that using her own body weight as resistance was hard work. In fact, she says, her arms had more definition after doing push-ups than when she was just lifting weights. The moral of the story: you don't need some high-tech gym with lots of equipment to start strength training.

If you don't have access to a gym or weight room, there are a number of ways to work on strength at home, with little or no equipment. The most important part of strength training is resistance — you have to find a way to build resistance, whether it's using your own body weight, a beach ball or a monster dictionary. Here are some suggestions for no-frills strength-training exercises that you can do at home:

Toe raises — calf muscles
Stand on a step on the balls of your feet, letting your heels hang over the edge of the step. Slowly lift your body by raising yourself up onto your toes, then lower yourself by letting your heels drop below the step. The motion should be slow and controlled. Try pointing your toes inwards, outwards and straight ahead to work different parts of the calf muscle. If you find you need more resistance, grab a dictionary (or something similar) to increase the weight that your legs are raising.

Lunges — quads, glutes, hamstrings
Lunge by stepping forward with one leg and bending your knees into a lunge position (so your knee is bent about ninety degrees). Lunge forward with one foot, then either return to starting position and switch legs, or push off of your back foot and move forward in a large stepping motion (this will cause the exercise to travel). The key is to not extend your front knee

51

past your foot, so make sure you take large steps. Keep your hands on your hips and watch your posture — you don't want to bend forward or arch your back. Keep your stomach and back muscles tight to work those muscles as well.

Wall sits — quadriceps, hamstrings, glutes

Wall sits are similar to squats or lunges, but they tend to put less pressure on your knees. To work your quads and glutes, stand with your back against a wall and bend your knees until they are parallel to the floor. It should look like you're sitting in an imaginary chair. Hold it . . . thirty seconds? One minute?

Step ups — quads, glutes

Stand facing a sturdy bench or platform (a picnic table bench is the perfect height). Step up first with your right foot, then your left, so you are standing on the bench. Then step back down with your right leg, then left. Pump your arms to get the movement going, and keep repeating.

Wall push-ups — arms, upper back, chest

A variation on the mighty-tough regular push-up, wall push-ups work the same way, but you're standing up and pushing against a wall. Stand a few steps back from the wall to put more pressure on your arms. Remember to keep your stomach tight as you do sets of five or ten reps. Try putting your hands in different positions on the wall to work different muscle groups: close together with your thumbs and forefingers forming a diamond to work your triceps, far apart to work your back and shoulders, or way down low on the wall or up high above, at head height.

Triceps dips — triceps

To get into position, sit on a sturdy bench or step with your legs stretched out in front of you, heels on the floor, feet flexed. Put your arms by your sides, and grip the bench so that your fingers curl over the front of the bench. Step your heels out forward as you push your torso up — you want to end up in what looks like a reverse push-up position. Now you're set to "dip." Your weight should be on your arms, and you want to lower your body (keeping it straight) by bending your arms until your upper arm is parallel with the ground, then lift your body back up by straightening your arms. If you're doing this move correctly, your elbows will bend behind you, and you will definitely feel those triceps burn!

Arm exercises with equipment

Investing in a pair of light barbells or a resistance band can take you far in the arm muscle department. Here are just a few exercises you can try with a lightweight (green) resistance band or a pair of two-, three-, or five-pound weights:

Biceps curls: Stand up straight with your feet shoulder-width apart, knees unlocked. Hold a barbell in each hand with your palms facing away from you, arms by your sides. The key is to keep your elbows glued to your sides as you bend your arms, lifting the barbells toward your shoulders. If you are using a resistance band, put the band under your feet and hold it in your hands as you would the weights. When you curl your arms toward your shoulders, you should feel resistance from the band or weights.

So you want to improve your . . .	Work your . . .	Try . . .
Jump shot	Legs and arms	High jump sequences, reaching as high as you can, over and over
Agility on the soccer field	Legs, endurance	Footwork drills — side-stepping cones, running tires
Far-reaching softball throw	Arms, shoulders, back	Wall and floor push-ups, with hands in varied positions
Sprinting time	Leg muscles	Running "suicides," where you sprint quick, short distances
Running distance	Endurance, leg muscles	Cardio exercises over a prolonged period of time at a lower intensity. Try slower jogs that take more time, and if you have to rest, keep walking (don't stop)
Straddle jump	Abductor (inner thigh) flexibility and quad strength	Straddle "stretches" and jumping sequences where you quickly kick out your legs
Swimming start	Legs — particularly quads and calves	Calf raises that end in a springy jump — roll through your whole foot

Triceps: Hold a light barbell over your head with one hand. Bend your arm so that you are reaching down your back with the weight. Your elbow should be pointed straight up in the air and as close to your head as possible. Keeping your elbow still, slowly raise and lower your hand to work the triceps. You can use your free arm to steady your working arm.

54

Chest Fly (pectorals): Stand with light barbells in either hand. Start with your arms outstretched at your sides, shoulder height, with your palms facing forward. Keep your arms slightly bent as you contract your stomach muscles and bring your arms together in front of you. It's almost as if you're hugging a big tree. Bring your arms back out to the sides and repeat. To do this exercise with a resistance band, wrap it around a sturdy pole or tree and grip the ends in your hands. Take a few steps away from the pole until you feel resistance. Turn your back to the pole and do the exercise as above.

Chest press with bouncing ball (pectorals): Hold a basketball-sized bouncing ball (like a beach ball) against your chest, arms bent, elbows out to the side. Your hands should be on either side of the ball, palms facing each other. The ball should be hard enough to provide resistance as you push on it from both sides. Push in and hold for a few seconds, then release. Repeat.

Easy ways to increase strength:

- Do light arm or leg exercises while talking on the phone or watching TV.
- Carry the groceries in from the car or home from the store (if they're light enough).
- Try cycling slowly with the resistance turned up, or walking on a steeply inclined treadmill.
- Practice good posture — hold your head up, tighten your stomach muscles, don't slouch.

Avoiding injury

One of the main reasons to concentrate on all three aspects of fitness (flexibility, endurance and strength) is to avoid getting hurt. Building a strong, healthy body means lessening your risk of injury, and building up your resilience — meaning you'll be better able to recover if you do get hurt. *During* exercise, there are a few guidelines to help avoid getting hurt:

● Warming up and cooling down will greatly decrease the chance of muscle aches and injury.

● Start any exercise program slowly; ease into it. This is especially true for strength training — always work with manageable weights, and start lighter than you think you have to.

● When weight lifting, use a spotter if you are unsure of your capabilities or feel particularly tired.

● Always listen to your coaches and teachers when they give safety tips.

● Wear proper clothing and protective gear. Always wear proper padding, head protection and appropriate shoes. When exercising outdoors or in the cold, make sure your clothing will keep your muscles warm.

No matter how many precautions we take, injuries still happen. If you do get injured, always consult a trainer if one is available. In cases where no one is available, most sports injuries — sprains and overused muscles — can be treated temporarily with a system called R.I.C.E., which stands for Rest, Ice, Compression and Elevation.

Rest means stop! Don't try to "run through" a sprained ankle or keep kicking goals with a swollen toe. Stop practicing and rest. Most sports injuries require a few days, if not weeks, of rest so consult a doctor about long-term effects. While you're resting, **ice** the injury. Icing decreases swelling, and is most effective when it immediately follows the injury. **Compressing** the injury also reduces swelling and can some-times stabilize weak muscles. Finally, **elevate** it — raise the injured area above your heart to decrease bleeding and swelling.

While R.I.C.E. is a good immediate treatment, most sports injuries require long-term attention, which can include simple exercise, more intensive rehabilitation exercises and treat-ments, or bandages and braces. If you want to rehabilitate the injury completely, it is important to follow through on proper treatment and take your doctor's advice. Don't be anxious to rush back into training too quickly, or you will put yourself at high risk for another injury or never healing correctly.

Katie Smith of the Minnesota Lynx is familiar with the pain and patience involved in injury. She has seriously damaged her knee, an injury she describes as

After rehabbing a knee injury during the 1999 and 2000 WNBA seasons, Rebecca Lobo was ready, willing and able to get back on the court. In fact, she spent the winter before the 2001 WNBA season playing professional hoops in Spain!

R and R

Leading an active, energized life is important, but even the most hardcore athletes know that rest and relaxation are essential from time to time. The season is pretty exhausting in the WNBA, so nearly all of the players take a few weeks off afterward to let their bodies rest. They also try to take breaks during the season. It's all about listening to your body, to recognize when it needs a break. If you get physically and emotionally exhausted (the usual culprits: not sleeping enough, working too hard or stress), you're more likely to get sick or injured, and your body certainly won't be at it's best performance-wise.

New York Liberty Becky Hammon is one athlete who listens to what her body needs. She says she's big on sleep, because, "More than anything, you gotta get a lot of rest. Your body's doing a lot of work for you out there and it's important to give it the proper rest."

"probably the hardest thing." Katie explains, "Just having to start from scratch in getting yourself back together — it's a little scary because you never know if you'll make it back to where you were." Luckily for Katie, her patience and hard work paid off, and her 2000 WNBA season was a wild success — she was awarded second team All-WNBA!

New York Liberty Rebecca Lobo is no stranger to injury, either. Rebecca spent all of the 1999 and 2000 seasons rehabbing her knee, focusing on strengthening her legs in order to prevent further injury. Throughout the season, she typically did three hours of strength training three times a week, plus an hour of cardio a day (like on non-impact stationary bikes), and a load of agility drills. Talk about dedication and patience!

Injuries are usually frustrating and painful, but staying positive and listening to your doctors and trainers can work wonders. Their advice *will* help you get better, as long as you follow it!

Guidance is golden

When WNBA players talk about their success, they usually agree on one thing: Somewhere along the line, they had strong mentors and good guidance. The women point to many coaches, players and trainers who have guided them through workouts, designed exercise programs and gotten their game in shape. That guidance was especially helpful to them when they were starting out. It is much harder to unlearn bad technique than it is to learn good technique and stick with it right from the start.

Rebecca Lobo says guidance is the most important thing for teens and kids who are starting to exercise or getting into athletics. A good coach can be invaluable when learning technique, game strategies and even healthy eating habits. And it's particularly helpful when starting a strength-training routine. "It's important to do strength training," Rebecca says, "but you need someone to teach you how to do it properly." Rebecca credits her college strength coach for teaching her how to lift weights properly. "When I was younger, I didn't have the proper form, and that's why I didn't get much stronger." College also matched Rebecca up with a nutritionist — a person who, she says, really helped her figure out what her body needs.

So what can you do if you don't have access to a strength coach or nutritionist? Orlando Miracle fitness whiz Adrienne Johnson recommends asking a lot of questions. Does your school have a nurse or gym teacher who know their stuff? Maybe there's a coach at a local gym or youth club who would be willing to talk to you. Or your doctor might be able give more general exercise advice or refer you to a colleague. Anyone you can find — ask them questions. They'll probably be happy to help. Also, read. A lot. There are tons of reputable books out there detailing proper form and technique.

Mental toughness

A lot of coaches talk about something called "mental toughness," as an important attribute for an athlete. This is a person's ability to withstand difficulties — both physical and mental — and it applies to all areas of life, not just athletics. It's the ability to bounce back and be resilient. A player who shows mental toughness is able to stay in control of her game and focus on what she needs to do in order to help her team, stay healthy and, of course, win.

Adrienne Johnson thinks that mental toughness is a learned trait. Adrienne feels that when you go through something difficult, it makes you stronger. She applies this belief to both her game and her life. Before both the 2000 and 2001 WNBA seasons, Adrienne trained at a high-pressure fitness program called L.G.E. Performance Systems. At L.G.E., she worked one-on-one with a trainer who developed a fitness regimen with her, constantly pushing her past her comfort zone in order to show Adrienne just how much she was capable of as an athlete.

"I'd be on the treadmill and just about hitting the wall," Adrienne explained, "when [my trainer] Pat would want to step it up. It was at that point that I had a decision to make. I could either say 'I can't do it,' or I could adjust and say 'I only have five minutes left, I'll do it.'" Adrienne would visualize herself chugging through those last few minutes, and it would work!

Intense training like Adrienne withstood is one sure way to build mental toughness, but it's not something that should be done without a qualified training expert. But you can learn from Adrienne's experience — knowing what you're capable of and believing in yourself is half the game. When Adrienne came back after her first season at L.G.E., she found she was a more confident player because she knew what her body was capable of doing. She set new scoring highs for herself, and was runner-up for the WNBA's most improved player award.

"Mentally, if you're not in the right state before a game, the physical isn't going to follow," Adrienne says. If you have confidence, you bring calmness to the court, which allows you to perform at your best level. Some athletes call it the "ideal performance state." That's when you're relaxed, confident, challenged, focused and alert.

Reaching this mental "zone" comes with experience. It takes hard work, time and dedication to have control over your mind and body. Katie Smith of the Lynx offers this advice about getting over pregame jitters: "I just stay focused, know that I've done this so many times, and just

Adrienne Johnson is one tough player on the court. But her game is not just about physical ability. She has confidence in herself, which means she is prepared to handle any situation that comes her way!

relax and play. All you can really control is yourself — just think about that, as opposed to all the things you don't have any control over." The ability to focus your thoughts comes with practice. The more you work on a sport or activity, the tougher you become mentally. As you develop a skill, you gain confidence, and with that confidence comes the knowledge that you can and will succeed. As you learn what your body is capable of, it becomes easier to push "I can't" out of your vocabulary.

Seeing Is Believing: Visualization

Many athletes practice a technique called *visualization*. It works exactly the way it sounds — you visualize yourself in the moment in order to prepare yourself mentally. A lot of WNBA players use visualization to prepare themselves for a game. Before the big event (the night before, or even a few hours or minutes before) they relax, visualizing themselves at the game staying confident and focused.

Adrienne Johnson takes about ten minutes the night before a game or pregame to relax, breathe deeply and visualize herself playing well. Adrienne likes to focus on her emotions — she says that if she can imagine herself staying cool and calm, then she is more likely to bring those emotions to the game.

Cleveland Rockers forward Rushia Brown credits a coach with teaching her to visualize and focus. "My college coach taught me to calm down for a little bit, think about all the things I need to do — just erase the rest of my day so I can prepare myself mentally." She physically prepares for a game with her teammates beforehand, but she also takes a few minutes alone prior to tip-off to get focused and ready.

Visualization techniques are used by many athletes, not just basketball players. Divers, for example, will often visualize themselves completing a perfect dive before they get on the board. Some believe that if they see themselves do a strong takeoff and a clean entry, they will perform that flawlessly in reality, too.

COMPONENTS OF PHYSICAL FITNESS

One of the most crucial elements of a tough mindset is resiliency — the ability to bounce back. You need to be able to put mistakes behind you and not get caught up on that one bad play or error. It isn't an easy skill to develop, but resiliency can be a huge asset to an athlete. Sure, you want to think about what you messed up in a game and work on it in practice. But if you get caught up in one missed pass during the game, your head isn't where it needs to be for that next rebound.

So practice hard and keep your head in the game — these are two great ways to build mental toughness. But most important, learn to stick with it (whatever sport or skill "it" is!). Making goals for yourself and seeing them through is a definite confidence builder. Also, talk to your coaches, gym teachers and any physical fitness experts whom you have access to. Ask a lot of questions so you can stay on top of your game and really understand the exercises or drills you are doing. Finally, as a word of caution, make sure you are working out at a level that is healthy for you, and check with a doctor if you're concerned.

How does she hit that shot? And how can I?!!

The player	The move	Why it's useful	Where does it come from?	How she enhances it	What you can do at home	Her comments
Kara Wolters Center Indiana Fever	Hook shot	It's unstoppable. You can block the defender with your left arm while shooting with your right.	Her dad taught it to her.	It's basically a motion Kara has had down since she was a kid, so it's second nature to her. But Kara is also an exercise queen, and loves the weight room. So she keeps her upper body strong, and that right arm is just golden!	Practice is the key for tough shots like this one. A big part of this move is the motion, which is easier to learn when you're young. So, practice, practice, practice.	"In high school, my dad, Willie, played against Kareem Abdul-Jabbar. He jokes that Kareem stole the move from him. Really, I stole it! Now whenever I play against Nykesha Sales, who I played with in college, she says 'Let's see that hook shot, Willie!'"
Jennifer Gillom Center Phoenix Mercury	Fade away jump shot	You can hit the shot even when you're being closely guarded.	"I really created the shot when I was younger, playing pickup with the guys. They just loved blocking shots, and I had to do something!"	Jennifer does lots of push-ups and leg exercises to keep her muscles strong. She'll get on her stationary bike and tighten the resistance to work her leg muscles.	Push-ups for your arms, and leg exercises. Try doing a series of jumps — it works your leg muscles and builds endurance!	"It's such an effective shot, going against the [Margo] Dydeks, who just tower over you . . . you can't stop the fade away jump shot."

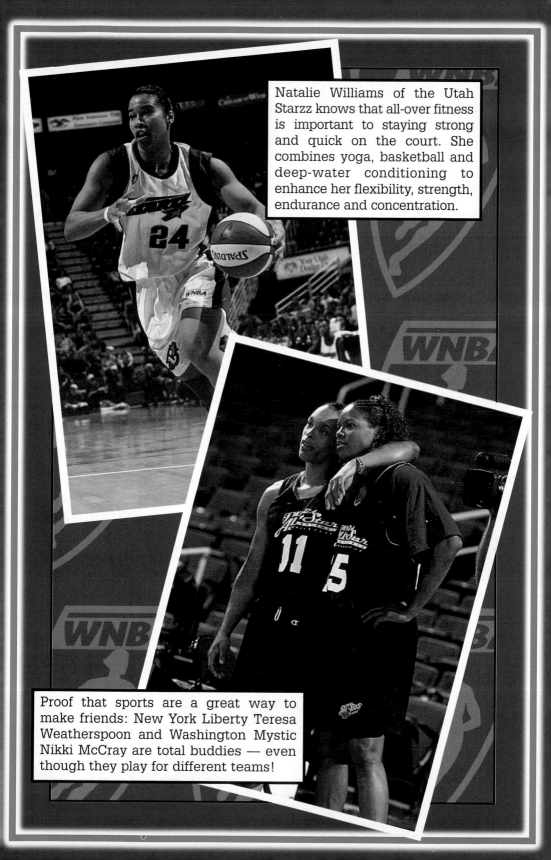

Natalie Williams of the Utah Starzz knows that all-over fitness is important to staying strong and quick on the court. She combines yoga, basketball and deep-water conditioning to enhance her flexibility, strength, endurance and concentration.

Proof that sports are a great way to make friends: New York Liberty Teresa Weatherspoon and Washington Mystic Nikki McCray are total buddies — even though they play for different teams!

Yolanda Griffith of the Sacramento Monarchs jumps above her opponents to make the shot! She stays on top by doing exercises that strengthen her leg muscles.

Off the court, the Los Angeles Sparks joke around together to build friendships and trust. On the court, that togetherness pays off as they rally together to play and win.

Charlotte Sting Dawn Staley knows it's important to be active both on and off the court. She spends her free time running a community foundation for inner-city kids and young adults.

Wendy Palmer of the Detroit Shock shares a joke with a teammate as she pushes herself on the bench press. Laughing helps Wendy pass the time in the weight room and makes getting fit fun!

Indiana Fever Kara Wolters says that practice and determination will help you reach your goals: "I am proof that you can do anything you set your mind to."

The Sacramento Monarchs celebrate a big win together after months of practice. They all know that pushing one another to work harder will make them better athletes. Teamwork really pays off in the end!

Minnesota Lynx star Katie Smith was a dancer as a kid — she took both ballet and tap dancing. Today, she uses what she learned as a dancer — footwork and leg strength — in her powerful performance on the basketball court.

Chamique Holdsclaw of the Washington Mystics knows it's important to keep exercise fun. She loves playing pick-up hoops with friends to keep herself in shape.

Brandy Reed of the Phoenix Mercury practices her shots until they're perfect. She knows that developing skills in practice will make her a more confident player during the game.

Miami Sol Debbie Black keeps water ready to replenish herself after a tough battle on the court. If you stay hydrated, your body will be ready for anything!

Warm-ups aren't just important to get your body prepped. Rushia Brown of the Cleveland Rockers says that during warm-ups, "I just erase the rest of my day so I can prepare myself mentally."

Houston Comet Tina Thompson concentrates on having fun as she does an "alternate workout" — shopping for a bargain is a major calorie-burner and stress-zapper.

Lisa Leslie of the Los Angeles Sparks and Houston Comets pal Tina Thompson are both over six feet tall and proud of every inch! When they're not bent over laughing together, they're standing straight and tall.

Be Active 2000 Spokeswoman Nykesha Sales throws punches for charity at a fund-raiser for breast cancer research. Nykesha loves working out — especially for a good cause. "Exercise doesn't have to be a chore!" she says.

BE ACTIVE

The WNBA is so concerned with health and fitness that it formed a partnership with Nike to help kids and teens stay in shape. The program, *Be Active,* presented by Nike, encourages you to "Play Fit, Stay Fit," by focusing on the three main areas of fitness: endurance, strength and flexibility.

Four of the WNBA's brightest stars are the spokeswomen for *Be Active 2001* — 2000 Olympic gold medalists Natalie Williams of the Utah Starzz and Katie Smith of the Minnesota Lynx, along with WNBA All-Stars Tina Thompson of the Houston Comets and Detroit Shock forward Wendy Palmer. They will carry on the healthy traditions started by the *Be Active 2000* spokeswomen — former Cleveland Rockers' leader Suzie McConnell-Serio; Cynthia Cooper, two-time MVP and former guard for the Houston Comets; Jennifer Gillom of the Phoenix Mercury and the Orlando Miracle's Nykesha Sales. The 2001 spokeswomen will travel the country promoting the *Be Active*, which tipped off in January 2000 just in time for start of the new millennium!

Be Active travels to different towns throughout the United States and presents 90-minute clinics for

Nykesha Sales, a spokeswomen for *Be Active 2000*, says that staying fit, for her, is not just about being a great athlete — it's about living a long healthy life. She feels so strongly about it, she even got her grandmother to start lifting light weights!

boys and girls ages 11-14. With the help of health and fitness professionals, WNBA stars teach participants all about fitness and nutrition, and why it's so important to get and stay active.

Lisa Leslie is the spokeswoman for the WNBA's partnership with Sears to promote breast cancer awareness. This is a cause Lisa cares about very much. What do you feel strongly about? Are there charities or organizations you would like to help out with?

Be Active spokeswomen discuss fitness for the first part of the clinic, and then everyone participates in fun activities that teach participants about health and fitness, stressing the idea that being active and getting in shape should *always* be fun. Sometimes a WNBA player will lead participants in drills or in her favorite exercise. Another activity might be a nutrition expert answering questions or presenting yummy, good-for-you snacks.

Jennifer Gillom, who led a lot of programs on the West Coast in 2000, really loved being a part of *Be Active*. "I didn't have this kind of guidance and knowledge growing up," Jennifer says. "And hearing myself speak, I realize how much I could have benefited from these types of clinics as a kid."

Be Active knows that it's important to get the word about fitness out early. The program is all about being positive and healthy, stressing the idea that exercise is fun, and practicing good nutrition doesn't have to be difficult. Taking care of your body and getting active will help you perform better in the classroom, gym, pool and on the field and court. It's *all* good.

Be Active clinics are held from January through August. At the start of the season the WNBA also celebrates National *Be Active* Week with lots of activities to promote health and well-being. Check out *Be Active*'s web site at wnba.com for more info — a clinic may be just what you need to jump-start your active, healthy lifestyle!

Active lives

Being active means a lot more than sports. It's important to be active in school, in your community and in everyday life, too. Living a healthy life means being involved in a range of different activities involving not only your physical self, but also activities that challenge your mind and spirit.

WNBA players get active in a variety of ways. For starters, they all have other hobbies outside of basketball. Some have families or other jobs. Sheryl Swoopes and Yolanda Griffith are both moms who keep basketball close to their hearts, but their children even closer. And Kate Starbird of the Utah Starzz is the founder of "3-Headed Cyclops," a 3-D animation studio that creates special effects and animations for commercials and films. In addition to ball handling for the Starzz, Kate handles advertising, finance and public relations for 3HC. Kate got her college degree in computer science, so she's happy to be able to keep up her techie side while still playing ball.

Other WNBA stars have charities or causes, like *Be Active*, that they are involved with or even manage. No doubt about it, helping people is a great way to build up your spirit!

The New York Liberty's Rebecca Lobo, for instance, runs in Race for the Cure, a yearly run that raises money for breast cancer research. Rebecca feels strongly about this event because her mother RuthAnn was diagnosed with breast cancer when Rebecca was in college. RuthAnn had a tough battle and ultimately won — she is now healthy. Rebecca knows it's important to keep supporting breast cancer research — it might some day lead to a cure!

Houston Comet Monica Lamb was the winner of the American Express Small Business Services 2000 WNBA Entrepreneurial Achievement Award. Monica really knows how to stay active. She founded a wellness program for women in 1998 called The Monica Lamb Foundation, which teaches women and children about health and wellness. The key to wellness, Monica says, is balance: "You're 'well' when you incorporate all the areas — your mind, your body and your spirit — and you just feel good about yourself."

Monica and Rebecca's volunteerism is a great way of being active in the community. But there are other, more private and personal ways to enrich your spirit, too.

In 2001, just her second WNBA season, Sylvia Crawley of the Portland Fire has proven that she is one active player. Athletically, Sylvia is at the top of her game. (Six-foot-five Sylvia could also earn a valuable place in history, since she's got an ace in her hand that wasn't brought out in 2000 but could get played anytime — she can dunk!) Basketball is so important to Sylvia that she spends her off-season as an assistant coach for North Carolina.

But Sylvia isn't only active on the court. In her free time,

Sylvia develops her hobby — poetry. Sylvia started writing around 1996, and soon realized that poetry came naturally to her, almost like dribbling the ball. Poetry is Sylvia's creative outlet, and something special she does for herself — in addition, of course, to wowing Portland fans on the court.

Like Kate, Rebecca, Monica, Sylvia and other well-rounded WNBA players, you too can find many ways to stay active within and outside of athletics. School, for one, is a pretty obvious answer. Being active in school is the most important thing you can do for yourself right now. Even if you don't get stellar grades, it's crucial to give it all you've got in the classroom. As long as you're learning and trying hard, you're enriching your mind — and that's a main part of total fitness!

So now that the academic thing is out of the way, what else can you do to enrich your mind? Getting involved in your school and community outside of the classroom is certainly one way to go. Joining school clubs, student government, volunteer organizations — these are all terrific ways to get involved, be active and round out your life. Just trying different activities or projects will help build new skills, and you might find you really love an activity you never even considered. Getting involved and leading an active life makes you a well-rounded individual. Besides, who wants to be bored all day?

School, religious and community clubs hold lots of different opportunities. Student government can teach great leadership and cooperation skills — not to mention bringing some of you shy gals out of your shells! Or maybe you've always thought you had a pretty decent singing voice when you're belting it out in the shower. Why not go out for your school's chorus? It's activities like these that will enrich your mind and spirit because they challenge you to do different things and meet new people.

It's important to be open to different ideas, and to be willing to try new activities. The more well rounded you are, the more options you'll have, and the more exciting your life will be! Maybe you're a great soccer player, but you've never picked up a paintbrush. Why not develop that secret artistic side of you that's just waiting to come out? You don't have to jump into impressionistic oil paints. Start small — try sketching in a notebook, or signing up for an introductory art class. Trying new things is one of the best ways you can guarantee that you'll stay active, enthusiastic and involved.

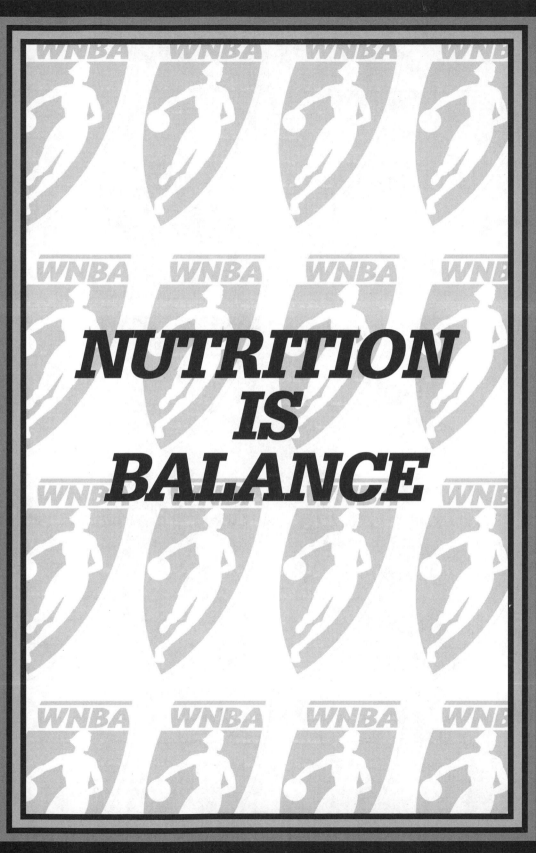

NUTRITION IS BALANCE

NUTRITION IS BALANCE

If you're like most people, you've probably spent a lot of time thinking about food. It's just a huge part of our culture. Think about the chips you devour while chilling with your friends, the popcorn you share on that oh-so-casual first date at the movies and the cafeteria food we all love to hate. And of course there's always the celebratory birthday cake. Food is everywhere — and it's a major part of our lives.

But food is more than culture. It's what gives us life. It provides energy, vitamins and nutrients — all major stuff. (And doesn't a double fudge caramel brownie sundae at the right time just make the world look a little brighter?) Eating right is one of the most important things you can do for your body, and it's important to develop good eating habits when you're younger.

Almost every athlete will tell you that her diet is super-important. Because athletes expend more energy than most people, they need to make sure they are getting enough calories and eating the right foods. Nikki McCray is totally careful about what she eats, because, she says, it impacts her game. "You can work out, you can run, you can lift all you want, but if you don't eat properly, I think that really plays a lot into your fitness — and your performance out on the court." Nikki is a big fan of eating carbohydrates before tipoff. Her favorite pregame meal is usually angel hair pasta with red sauce, because it gives her the energy she needs to play hard and keep herself focused on the game — not on her stomach.

You've heard it a hundred times: three meals a day is key. Your body needs a certain amount of nutrients, and skipping meals is an instant way to lessen your chance of getting

all the good stuff. If you're rolling your eyes right now thinking *I am SO not a morning person*, well — I'm talking to you.
Take it from Rebecca Lobo, a self-proclaimed "breakfast girl."
"If I'm in a rush, I'll have a bowl of cereal and a piece of fruit.
But I like to have eggs, usually an egg white omelet. I've
always been a big breakfast girl, so if I skip breakfast, I'm
hurting the rest of the day."

Breakfast is one of the easiest eating habits to get into.
Way too many people skip that oh-so-important first meal of
the day — for no good reason. Breakfast gives your body the
A.M. fuel it needs to function, keeping you alert and better
able to focus and concentrate. Eggs, orange juice, cereal,
French toast . . . even a quick banana and a handful of granola
is better than nothing. Breakfast provides that burst of energy you need to hold you till lunch. After all, who wants to go
through the eternity known as science class on an empty
stomach?

Super-quick breakfast treats to jump-start your day:

- English muffin with peanut butter
- Bananas or melon with cottage cheese
- Real fruit smoothie with frozen yogurt
- Cereal with chopped fruit or berries
- Waffles are not for syrup alone . . . add fruit like straw-
berries and bananas on top for a special treat!

(Hint: Pair these quick treats up with a glass of OJ and/or
lowfat milk and you're on your way to a healthy day!)

RECIPE: Fruit Smoothie

Ingredients:

- **2 cups frozen fruit (berries and/or bananas work well)**
- **1 cup juice (orange, pineapple or lemonade are good choices)**
- **1 cup vanilla yogurt (or get creative with flavored yogurt)**

Peel the banana and freeze the fruit. If you don't have time to freeze the fruit, you can add ice directly into the blender instead. Add fruit, juice and yogurt into the blender and blend until smooth. Serve.

Hint: Experiment with different combinations of fruits, juices and amounts of ice to create different flavors and textures.

The C word

Calories. It can sound like such a bad word. *That dessert is so high in calories. Steer clear of high-calorie foods. Are you watching your calorie intake?* Listening to some people talk, you would think that calories are weapons of mass destruction. Reality check: a calorie is a unit of energy. Pretty harmless, really. Calories are energy that you need Need NEED to survive. And as a child or teen, your body requires energy to grow and develop. Experts recommend that teen girls consume about 2,200 calories a day, though if you're really active, you probably need more. If you look on food labels, you'll notice that most daily allowance percentages are based on a 2000-calorie diet (in fewer cases, 2500 calories), so you should adjust accordingly.

If you're an athlete, burning up lots of energy on the court, the field or in the pool, you need to take in more calories than the average person. And it is doubly important for you to make sure you're eating balanced meals (and not just a ton of sugar!), otherwise you won't be getting the right kinds of foods. You'll miss all the vitamins, minerals and complex carbohydrates your body needs to perform at its best.

Food is the fuel that keeps the Utah Starzz Natalie Williams performing at top levels. She tries to eat every four hours, because, she says, "Being so active, it really keeps your metabolism going." Not that Natalie is chowing down on fast food and candy all day long. "I just eat in moderation," she says. "I eat a lot of protein and carbs together, and I always drink a lot of water. You can eat sweets, but just in moderation."

The food pyramid — you've seen it a million times, but do you pay attention?

The Food Guide Pyramid comes from the U.S. Department of Agriculture / Health and Human Services and gives us a guide for what people need to eat to stay healthy. But how many people truly pay attention to it? Do you? Are you eating three to five servings of vegetables every day? Maybe you're groaning at the very thought. But read on, and be enlightened on how to make those three to five servings seem like cake. (It might have to be carrot cake, but you get the idea.)

First off, notice the largest area of the pyramid, down at the bottom — the **bread, cereal, rice and pasta group**. Lately it's become fashionable to cut out these carbs (carbohydrates)

NUTRITION IS BALANCE

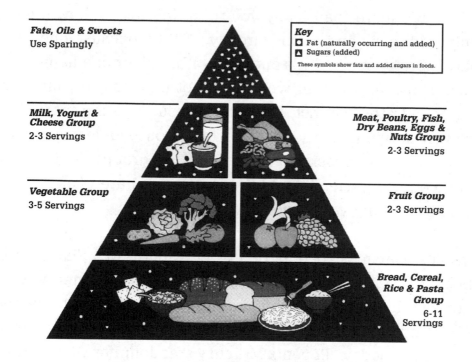

Fats, Oils & Sweets
Use Sparingly

Key
☐ Fat (naturally occurring and added)
▲ Sugars (added)
These symbols show fats and added sugars in foods.

Milk, Yogurt & Cheese Group
2-3 Servings

Meat, Poultry, Fish, Dry Beans, Eggs & Nuts Group
2-3 Servings

Vegetable Group
3-5 Servings

Fruit Group
2-3 Servings

Bread, Cereal, Rice & Pasta Group
6-11 Servings

to lose weight. This is *not* a good weight loss plan for teens. In fact, cutting out all of any food group is not healthy. (You're thinking that's crazy, right? That there's an exception? The three-letter word that rhymes with "bat," right? Wrong. Even FAT has its place in a healthy diet.)

The bread and grain group is the biggest box on the chart. That's because you need six to eleven servings of the stuff every day. Why so much? Because this food group, which is high in carbohydrates, provides most of your body's energy. Every group on the chart provides some fuel, but carbs are your body's *preferred* source — meaning you will burn this kind of food first. Luckily, the bread group is probably the easiest to come by — think bread, bagels, rolls, rice, macaroni, corn flakes, crackers, muffins . . . you get the idea.

It's more than likely you're eating six to eleven servings of breads and grains already. That's because one serving is pretty small — it's one slice of bread, or one half-cup of rice or pasta. In other words, it's not hard to get your fill of carbohydrates. In fact, if you think you're eating more than eleven servings of the bread group, you should make sure that you're not missing out on other food groups — like fruits and veggies. (Ahem! And the last time you ate your broccoli was how many years ago?)

Speaking of fruits and veggies, these are the two food groups that most people don't get enough of. Shame, too, because they not only provide your body with energy, they are also loaded with vitamins, minerals, carbohydrates and fiber. It is important to have two to four servings of the **fruit group** every day. Phoenix Mercury star Jennifer Gillom has a great suggestion for adding fruit into your diet. She says that if she's craving dessert, she'll try to eat something with in it. That way she's satisfying her sweet tooth and eating healthy!

The **vegetable group** is similar to fruit. (But who wants to eat *them* as dessert?) They also provide essential vitamins, minerals, carbohydrates and fiber. You've got to up the intake, though, to three to five servings every day. That's not really so bad, when you realize that one serving is about one cup of salad or half a cup of chopped veggies (a small side-order size). And veggie pizza — hey, it counts! So does yummy stir-fry . . .

Moving up the chart, there's the **milk, yogurt and cheese group** — the dairy world. This group provides calcium,

RECIPE: Mini Vegetable Pizzas

Ingredients:

- ◯ **English muffin, pita bread or mini pizza bread**
- ◯ **Tomato (or "pizza") sauce**
- ◯ **1 handful of shredded cheese (mozzarella is most common, but any cheese will do)**
- ◯ **Chopped up veggies of your choice (Some popular favorites? Peppers, mushrooms, broccoli — use your imagination!)**
- ◯ **Optional spices: Oregano, garlic powder, crushed red pepper (for the spice girls among us!)**

Spread tomato sauce onto bread and top with shredded cheese. Arrange your chopped veggies on top and sprinkle with spices, if desired. Toast your pizza in a toaster oven until cheese is melted and muffin is browned (or for about 8-10 minutes in a 350° oven).

a major nutrient that you need, especially when your bones are developing (since women's bones continue to grow well into our early twenties, you probably fit in this category). According to the chart, you need at least two to three servings of dairy a day, though the U.S. Food and Drug Administration says that should be a bit higher for teens — three or more servings a day of calcium-rich foods is recommended, and some dietitians say four servings is ideal. Some painless ways to down the dairy? Cereal with one cup of milk (a great morning starter), a cup of yogurt (toss in some granola or cereal if you're craving texture) or pizza.

Ditto that two to three daily servings for the next section on the chart — the **meat group**. For those of you who don't like to eat a lot of red meat, fish, eggs and chicken count, too. This group provides protein, which gives your body amino acids to keep body tissue healthy. Protein is super-important for muscle growth and as a source of energy. If you work out a lot and don't get enough protein, your muscles could eventually start burning themselves for energy — not a good thing. You can make sure you're getting your protein by eating a variety of foods (no, you're not limited to meat!) including seeds and nuts, beans, fish and eggs. One serving of this group may actually be less than you think — one egg is a serving, as is just two handfuls of peanuts or sunflower seeds (about 1/3 of a cup).

The last food group on the chart is **fats, oils and sweets**. And no, unfortunately, it's not at the top because it's the most important. It's way up there because it's the group we're supposed to eat the least amount of. "Use sparingly" is the key phrase, actually. Most Americans eat way too much of this category (think candy, the grease of fried foods and fat). Eating too much saturated fat (the kind that comes from animal fat and hydrogenated vegetable oils) can increase cholesterol levels and therefore increase the risk of heart disease. Because high cholesterol can be especially risky later in life, it's good to start practicing positive eating habits early on.

But notice that the food chart doesn't say "Cut out sweets and fats entirely." Like all the other food groups, fats are a necessary part of a healthy diet. That's why they're on the chart. For one, fat helps transport vitamins and minerals through your body. Many vitamins, like A, D, E and K, are fat-soluble (as opposed to water-soluble), so they use fat to move them through your blood to where they are needed. Fat is also a highly concentrated source of energy — more so than carbs or protein. One gram of carbohydrate or protein contains four calories of energy. A gram of fat, on the other hand, contains nine calories. As you know, your body stores fat (all bodies have to!) so that you will always have a concentrated energy supply on reserve. It makes sense when you think about it.

So if fat is so necessary, why does it seem like everyone's telling you to cut it out? Because most people eat too much of the stuff. You shouldn't cut out *all* the fat in your diet, you just don't want to eat too much of it. Nobody wants you to stop eating your favorite food just because it's not the healthi-

Ways to lessen your fat intake that won't break you!

⬤ Don't pile on the cream cheese, butter or salad dressings — you don't need it to be an inch thick to taste it!

⬤ Experiment with "part skim" or lowfat cheeses — you might not be able to tell the difference!

⬤ Keep cut up veggies around for snacking so you don't devour an entire bag of chips.

⬤ Try reduced-fat mayo — especially in chicken, egg and tuna salad.

⬤ If you drink whole milk, try 2%. If you already drink 2%, try 1%. And if you're at 1%, why not make the leap to skim?

⬤ Skip fruit canned in heavy syrup and try the fresh stuff instead.

Even the toughest WNBA stars have their weaknesses . . .

WNBA player	Sinful snack
Vicky Bullett	Ice-cream sandwiches. "I would eat those things 24-7."
Jennifer Gillom	Chocolate. "I definitely get the craving!"
Nikki McCray	French fries. "I'll eat McDonald's on the road."
Rebecca Lobo	Ice cream. "Might not be good for the body, but it's good for the soul."
Tina Thompson	Dessert. "I am not that big a junk food eater, but sometimes I do fall short to desserts!"

est thing in the world. The truth is, cutting out any one food, let's say potato chips, will probably make you crave it all the more. You'll either end up breaking your promise to cut it out and chow down a whole bag of chips in five minutes, or you'll find a substitute ("Well, maybe no potato chips, but I never said anything about Cheez Doodles . . ."). Instead of totally cutting out a food, it's a better idea to watch your overall diet, and gradually lessen your intake of high-fat or sugar foods, or sub-

---

RECIPE: Ants on a Log

Ingredients:
- Celery
- Peanut butter
- Chocolate chips and/or raisins

Take a clean stalk of celery and spread the inside with peanut butter. Add chocolate chips or raisins on top to make your "ants on a log."

---

stitute a healthier option at times — like baked corn chips with salsa, or a piece of fruit.

One WNBA player who understands the importance of eating in moderation is Rebecca Lobo. She doesn't believe in cutting out any one food. Instead, she says, it's a degree thing. "Instead of having three pieces of pizza, I'll have two. Or instead of two scoops of ice cream, I'll have one. That way you don't have the cravings. You can satisfy them without going overboard." But Rebecca also knows that because she is an athlete, she needs more food and energy than less-active people. So she rarely cuts down on any one food during the in-season. "You're working so hard that you just need to eat a lot," she says.

All six groups on the food pyramid are important in their own way. The key is balance, because the groups work together and rely on one another to work properly. Dietitian Lisa Tartamella, MS, RD, of the Yale New Haven Hospital, says the food pyramid is important because it encourages you to eat a variety of foods in the correct proportions. "A balanced diet is only balanced when it includes all of the food groups," Tartamella says. "There isn't one perfect food that you can eat all of the time — they all work together." She likes to compare a healthy body to a well-oiled machine. "Eating a balanced diet is like putting high-octane gasoline into your car. Without fuel, you won't go anywhere."

Dangers of dieting

You now know that cutting out any one food is not always the best idea. Want to know what's even worse? Cutting out whole food groups, or whole meals. In the age of fad diets, let this be a beacon in the storm for you — most diets are just not healthy. According to Tartamella, there is no advantage to fad diets, and they can have terrible effects. Even moderate dieting at too young an age can be hazardous, she says.

"People who chronically diet never develop a healthy relationship with food," Tartamella says. And this unhealthy mindset can cause stress, low self-esteem and even disordered eating. Even for people who are actively trying to lose weight, food is not the enemy. Food is necessary for survival, and should be viewed as a positive thing. It's a source of energy, life and (prepare yourself for cheesiness) happiness.

New York's Sue Wicks agrees that a healthy outlook on food is crucial. Eating healthy is very important to her, not just as an athlete, but as a woman. "I always try and eat the right way and eat enough good food," Sue says. "I think that's important. Everyone thinks 'just eat less,' but I think you just need to eat very good, healthy things. It's not just being thin — it's being healthy."

NUTRITION IS BALANCE

When Indiana Fever player Kara Wolters was a teen, she thought that the less she ate, the better. But she was overweight, and that attitude wasn't helping her. After high school, she realized she had to start watching her nutrition — not cutting out food, just making healthier choices. "It sounds strange," she says, "but I lost a lot of the extra weight by eating a lot. I try to eat every three hours to keep my metabolism going, because I'm really active and I need to eat to support that. I cut down my sugar intake and started eating more protein, fruits and vegetables. I haven't cut out carbs either, though — I just try to eat them in the morning and afternoon so they provide me with energy throughout the day, instead of late at night."

Having a healthy diet, like Kara, and "dieting" are two

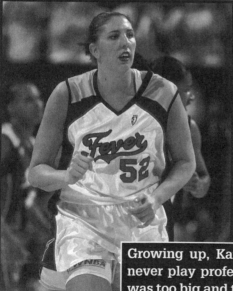

completely different things. In fact, some say that teens should cut the word "dieting" from their vocabulary altogether. Having a healthy diet means eating a variety of foods to get all the nutrients your body needs, while eating less-nutritious foods in moderation. "Dieting" on the other hand,

Growing up, Kara Wolters was told that she would never play professional basketball. "Everyone said I was too big and too slow. But I wouldn't be here today if I listened . . . I am proof that you can do anything you set your mind to."

means cutting things out that your body craves, limiting your overall intake of food, and always watching what you eat. Dieting is not a healthy option for most teens and preteens, unless it is done very carefully and with the help of a doctor or nutritionist. That's partly because your body is still growing, and not giving your body the energy and nutrients that it needs now will affect your development and growth.

At best, fad diets and the use of diet aids (such as pills) are temporary solutions. They rarely work, because you are likely to put back on the weight you lost as soon as you go off the diet. And Tartamella says they can be dangerous to your health, possibly even life threatening. They can slow or stop your growth, cause hair loss and gallstones, stop menstruation and weaken your bones by not allowing them to absorb the calcium they need. Fad dieting can also develop into an eating disorder, which can be extremely dangerous and life threatening.

Instead of fad diets where you cut out meals or certain food groups, or taking diet pills (another serious danger), what can you do if you need to lose weight? All you probably have to do is adjust your eating habits a little and follow the food pyramid. Make sure you're getting enough fruits and veggies and aren't wasting calories on too many sweets or fatty foods. When evaluating an eating plan, Tartamella tells her patients, "If you can't see yourself eating this way for the rest of your life, it's a diet and you shouldn't do it." Before considering any weight loss plan, you should talk to a trusted adult or a professional — it may be that you don't need to lose weight at all (for example, your body might be prepping itself for a growth spurt).

Eating Disorders

Eating disorders, like anorexia nervosa (deliberate self-starvation), bulimia nervosa (recurring binge eating and self-induced vomiting) and compulsive overeating are all serious emotional illnesses that have the potential to be fatal. Add to that list the newer illness known as "disordered eating," a term coined by the American College of Sports Medicine to cover compulsive or recurring eating problems that don't fit specifically into one of the above categories. None of these illnesses are something to play around with or take lightly. If you suspect that you or any one of your friends may be at risk, talk to a trusted adult immediately. The following are just a few warning signs of possible eating disorders:

- Intense fear of weight gain or extreme concern with body weight and shape.

- Bingeing on food and then purging (through vomiting, excessive exercise, use of laxatives, diet pills or diuretics).

- Refusal or inability to maintain minimal normal body weight for height and age.

- A loss of three consecutive menstrual periods.

While it is best to talk to someone you know, you can get additional information at the Eating Disorders Awareness and Prevention, Inc. Web site: **www.edap.org**, or at their toll free number **1-800-931-2237**.

A healthy alternative to dieting is to make sure you are active. In addition to eating balanced, healthy meals, you need to exercise if you want to tone up. The majority of teens don't need to diet, they need regular activity. And not crazy-intense spinning classes five times a week, either. Most teens and preteens just need to add more daily activity into their lives — more walking and running (and less TV time). The American College of Sports Medicine recommends moderate exercise, which they define as twenty minutes or more of aerobic activity, three to five days a week. If you're thinking of changing your eating or exercise habits any more than that, you should consult a doctor or school nurse.

Many girls have the opposite problem of chronic dieters. They want to bulk up, gain weight and fill out. The answer, again, is not to adopt extreme eating habits. Eating a ton of fat and sugar does not mean you will fill out in "all the right places." It just means you're taking in a lot of fat and sugar, which is not a healthy solution. If you think you are too skinny, you can try adding some shape to your body through exercise — toned muscles could give your body more definition. Moderate exercise and good eating habits will result in a healthier body, and healthy *is* more attractive.

Some food essentials . . . Power of protein

Jennifer Gillom says she had a weight problem all her life. She ate a lot of junk food, believing she would stay healthy because she exercised all the time. Then something clicked a few years ago, and she realized that she had to start paying better attention to her diet. Jennifer took a close look at what she was eating, and realized that she was loading up on carbs, and not getting nearly enough protein. So she adjusted. She started eating more dairy and meat, and a ton of vegetables.

"I felt much better and I lost a lot of weight that I didn't need," says Jennifer. "It definitely increased my endurance, though I did lose strength. I was big all my life, and had relied on that for strength and power. But while I lost some strength, I was quicker, and had more endurance. My whole game changed, and it extended my career."

Paying attention to what you eat is crucial, as Jennifer knows. Everything has to be in balance, so it's definitely a mistake to load up on carbs without getting enough protein. Meat and dairy are the biggest sources of protein, but it's also found in nuts, soy, peanut butter, dried beans and peas.

Protein is necessary for everyone — but especially active individuals who are

Jennifer Gillom snacks on a protein bar for a boost of energy. While these quick-fix snacks are great before a workout, Jennifer also incorporates a lot of protein, fruits and vegetables into her diet for everyday energy.

strengthening and toning their bodies. According to the American Dietetic Association (ADA), protein helps muscles contract, and we've already talked about how protein keeps body tissue healthy (by providing amino acids). It's a great energy source and muscle-builder. This explains why Jennifer felt more energy for longer periods of time when she got her protein and carbohydrates ratio in balance. Of course, you'll eat more carbs than protein (carbs are in just about everything, after all!) but make sure you're giving protein its due.

Houston Comet Tina Thompson prides herself on what she eats. She doesn't eat too many fried foods, and isn't a big junk food eater. Instead, she says, she eats well, including a lot of fruits, vegetables and protein. She loves eating chicken with a ton of vegetables, because, she says, it totally helps her game. Without the protein, she claims she couldn't get through her workouts — which are primarily cardio (the non-impact EFX is her favorite machine) because it helps her build up endurance. Both the way Tina eats and the cardio-vascular exercise she does are necessary for her as an athlete. One helps the other and, as a result, they both help her on the court. "When you maintain a certain level of endurance, it helps you be consistent on the court," she says. And if Tina is one thing, it's consistently strong.

Calcium and your bones, perfect together

There are 206 bones in the human body. They support us, protect us, give us shape and form and allow us movement. Your skeleton is really not something you want to mess with. But sadly, weak bones are getting to be a common phenomenon, particularly among women. Unfortunately, it's pretty easy to develop weak bones if you don't eat correctly as a teen and preteen. You are building up the bulk of your bone mass right now — and once your bones stop growing, you've lost most of your chance to strengthen them. So start thinking about your bones now. Seriously. They're your main support system, after all.

As you probably know from the milk ads, calcium is mucho important for building strong bones. Women are at an especially high risk for developing osteoporosis later in life if we don't get enough calcium when we're younger (osteoporosis is a disease that weakens your bones). Main bone growth occurs during puberty, though your bones will probably continue to develop and harden into your twenties. This is the time to load up on calcium — and it's really not much time, if you think about it. During puberty, your bones are growing like crazy and, conveniently, during this time, your body is also better able to absorb calcium — the rate of absorption is higher than it will be for the rest of your life. Calcium adds strength and stiffness to bones, helping in the growth process. As bones lengthen, they fill with calcium-rich minerals. After you hit a certain age, though, you will never be able to absorb calcium as well again, and your bones will eventually stop strengthening.

You know you can get calcium from dairy products, like milk, yogurt and cheese. But you can also find calcium in other foods, like grains, veggies and even in that "fats and sweets" category at the top of the food chart. Calcium is all over the place, so you should definitely pay attention to the Food and Drug Administration nutrition labels. Note though, that the recommended daily allowance on those labels is 1,000 milligrams. Between the ages of nine and eighteen, you'll need closer to 1,300 milligrams. A small glass of milk will give you about 30% of the "daily value" for calcium. Take that and a cup of yogurt (35%) and you've got 65% of the DV — you're halfway there. Your DV percentage of calcium should total 130%, because you need 1,300 mg instead of 1,000.

If you have problems digesting dairy, or are lactose-intolerant, make sure you're getting your share of lactose-reduced or lactose-free calcium-rich products. Also, pay attention to the chart on the next page that shows many non-dairy sources of calcium.

Some other great ways of getting calcium include calcium-fortified orange juice, multi-grain cereals and soy milk.

Health tip! An interesting fact about calcium- and vitamin-fortified cereals: because the added nutrients are often sprayed onto the cereal, they may get washed off into the milk. So don't skip that milk at the bottom of your cereal bowl — it could contain those extra nutrients you bought the cereal for in the first place!

Calcium in Strange Places		
Food serving	milligrams of calcium	percentage of FDA 's daily value (should total 130% every day)
2 waffles	200 mg	20% DV
1 cup lasagna	250 mg	25% DV
1/4 cup dry roasted almonds	100 mg	10% DV
1 stalk broccoli	60 mg	6% DV
1/2 cup collards	200 mg	20% DV
3 corn tortillas	80 mg	8% DV
1/2 cup pudding	100 mg	10% DV

Calcium, calcium, calcium. You get it — strong bones. But one more thing. Calcium won't do you much good unless you're also taking in vitamin D, because D helps your body absorb the calcium. You get vitamin D through the sun (normal daily exposure, not bake-like-a-potato exposure), and (surprise, surprise!) you drink it in most milks. That's why milk is such an ideal food — calcium and Vitamin D all in one.

To develop strong bones, it is also important to exercise. When you stretch and contract your muscles during exercise, growing bones will respond by becoming stronger and denser. Moderate exercise is ideal, so naturally, sports are great. But just being active will also help — swimming, walking the dog, carrying groceries. All help build stronger bones.

If you can strengthen your bones, you can of course weaken them, too. (You knew this was coming.) Alcohol and cigarette smoking are major ways to potentially damage building bones. Alcohol can cause your body to absorb less magnesium and zinc, not to mention calcium, all of which are necessary for bone development. Cigarette smoke is toxic to bone, and it can lessen your stamina, which will in turn affect your exercise routine. Skipping meals can also be harmful to bone growth because you're giving your body less chance to pick up the necessary nutrients. Eating disorders are just a more severe extension of that — they are a surefire way to upset your body's growth and development.

Some experts believe there is another, less obvious reason for weakened bones — excessive exercise or sports that put too much pressure on growing bones. Sports like long-distance running and gymnastics are constantly pounding on

"Got milk?"

Milk. You've seen the commercials. Maybe you tolerate it, maybe you drink a glass every night before bedtime. If so, great. But if you're one of those girls who can't stand the stuff, you're missing out — big time. And not just on all the bone benefits. Milk does a body good for a number of reasons, and you'll want to incorporate some into everyday life after you hear the stats.

 Milk means . . . a great smile. It's got lots of calcium and the vitamin D your body needs to absorb calcium. Calcium is stored in your teeth and is used for on-the-spot repairs to damaged tooth enamel.

 Milk means . . . healthy skin. Like water, milk hydrates you, cleaning your system, keeping cells and organs (like your skin) hydrated.

 Milk means . . . strength. Milk contains protein that helps build strong muscles.

 Milk means . . . less fat. Skim milk is fat free, but contains all the same nutrients as whole milk. If you're not skim style, 8 oz. of 1% lowfat milk has only 2 grams of fat.

 Milk's in . . . yummy foods like pudding, ice cream, scrambled eggs and custard.

your legs, which can be very stressful to your bones. Dietitian Lisa Tartamella says that because these athletes exert a lot of constant pressure on their bones, if they don't get enough calcium, they are much more likely to get stress fractures (small cracks) in their bones. It's important to wear proper shoes and equipment to protect yourself if you are active in a sport like this. And make sure to pay close attention to any warning signs your body may give you. Injuries should never be ignored or taken lightly.

Vitamins and minerals . . . do what?

Vitamins and minerals are terms we throw around a lot but rarely define. *You have to get your vitamins —* we all know that. But why? What are they really? And what does your body do with them? Answer: a lot of things. Different vitamins and minerals have different uses. In general, they help your body perform its functions. In the box on the next page are a number of common vitamins and minerals and the functions they perform.

The skinny on supplements

According to Tartamella, most active teens shouldn't need to take vitamin supplements. Assuming you're getting enough calories from a variety of foods, you're probably absorbing all the vitamins you need from that food. And that's great — because getting vitamins from a balanced diet is the ideal way to get your fill. Vitamin supplements, while they might sound like a no-brainer, don't always provide you with everything you need. There are nutrients in food, called "phytochemicals," that you can't get in a supplement. Also, supplements don't always provide the right mix of vitamins. Taking vitamins in certain combinations (combos often found naturally in food) helps your body absorb them. You've already heard about how calcium needs vitamin D to get absorbed. Another example is iron, which is most easily absorbed from animal products. Your body probably won't absorb an iron supplement as well, though you can increase the absorption by taking it with vitamin C.

There's another risk to vitamin supplements — the vitamins themselves. Taken in excess, many vitamins can actually be harmful. Every vitamin has a certain limit that's considered healthy (it varies for different people), and overdoing it can be very dangerous. Without advice from a doctor, you're probably safer sticking to food as your source for vitamins to avoid the risk of taking super high doses that may be dangerous.

Vitamin/Mineral	Found in	Purpose
A	Egg yolk, margarine, deep yellow vegetables like carrots and pumpkins	Fights infection, maintains healthy eyes, skin and hair
B2 (Riboflavin)	Almonds, cheese, eggs	Converts food to energy
C	Citrus fruits, tomatoes, strawberries, peppers	Strengthens bones, heals cuts and bruises, helps resist infection
D	Milk, egg yolk, salmon	Helps body absorb calcium to build strong bones and teeth
E	Nuts, vegetable oil, leafy green veggies	Defends against infection, forms and protects blood cells, muscles and nerves
Iron	Meat, shellfish, eggs, nuts, dried fruit	Transports oxygen, forms red blood cells, may protect against the effects of stress
Magnesium	Unprocessed foods like certain nuts and grains	Helps heart, muscles and nervous system, works with calcium to build bones and teeth
Potassium	Potatoes, bananas, raw veggies	Regulates heart rhythm, converts food to energy
Zinc	Shellfish, meat, seafood, cereal	Compose enzymes that help with various functions, including growth, skin and sense of taste

Health tip! If you're cooking for yourself, why not prepare a large chef's salad? It takes almost no prep time — you just need to buy the ingredients. The basic contents are lettuce, tomatoes, chopped up meat (ham, salami), sliced hard-boiled egg and shredded cheese. You can add in any kind of vegetables — broccoli, carrots, peppers, etc. Top with croutons if desired, and then your favorite salad dressing. *Voilà* — you've got nearly all the food groups represented in one dish!

Vegging out

Lots of teens and adults go the veggie route. According to the American Dietetic Association, that's totally cool, because vegetarian diets are healthful and nutritionally adequate when carefully planned. Did you catch that? The key phrase in that sentence is *when carefully planned.* That means if you're cutting out animal products, you have to be très careful not to cut out any necessary nutrients.

It's not easy being a vegetarian. In fact, it takes a lot more planning and flexibility to eat healthy, because you have to make sure you're getting the good stuff you need. You have to be willing to try new foods, and be open to different vegetables (translation: If you hate everything green, you might want to rethink your decision). A balanced vegetarian diet consists of a variety of foods, complete with lots of different fruits and vegetables. And you have to choose your calories wisely. Just because you're not eating meat does not give you free reign on the candy aisle. Sweets are low in nutritional value, so you don't want to waste your calories on them.

What specifically should you look out for when planning a vegetarian lifestyle? A couple of basics:

Calories: Vegetarian teens are at a slightly higher risk than most for not getting enough calories a day. That's because a vegetarian diet is typically lower in fat and full of fiber, so you might feel fuller faster — without actually eating enough calories. During the "growing years," this can be an especially serious danger. So if you're going veggie, make sure you're getting enough energy!

Protein: Fish and eggs are major sources of protein, but if you've cut them out or if you're a vegan (no animal products whatsoever), you can still get your body's share through plants. Some sources? Soy (but you probably knew that already!), grains, seeds, nuts and certain veggies. But don't just pick one food to fill your protein needs! It's important to shake up your diet, making sure that your protein is coming from a variety of sources.

Calcium: This one's a biggie, especially for vegans. Vegetarians have it a little easier, because you can still get plenty of calcium through dairy products like milk, cheese and yogurt. In fact, some studies have shown that vegetarians actually retain *more* calcium than their carnivorous counterparts. But if you're a vegan, or if you don't get enough dairy, you'll need to load up on dark-green vegetables like broccoli and spinach and calcium-fortified juices.

NUTRITION IS BALANCE

Vitamin B-12: This vitamin is naturally found solely in animal products. If you eat chicken or fish, you're probably okay. But if you're a strict vegetarian or vegan, you'll need to find some Vitamin B-12-fortified foods. There are lots out there, like soy milk and special cereals. And vitamin supplements are always an option, when used correctly.

Iron: Some vegetarians may not get enough iron in their diet, because the major sources of this nutrient are red meat, liver and egg yolk. But there are also plant sources that provide iron — like beans, spinach and dried fruits.

A word of caution: Some nutrients can actually be harmful if you take too much of them (as in vitamin supplements). You should consult a nutritionist, school nurse or responsible adult to help you plan a vegetarian diet. Also, you might want to pick up a book or two on becoming a vegetarian — there are lots of helpful guides out there, and the added bonus is that they usually contain tons of tasty recipes.

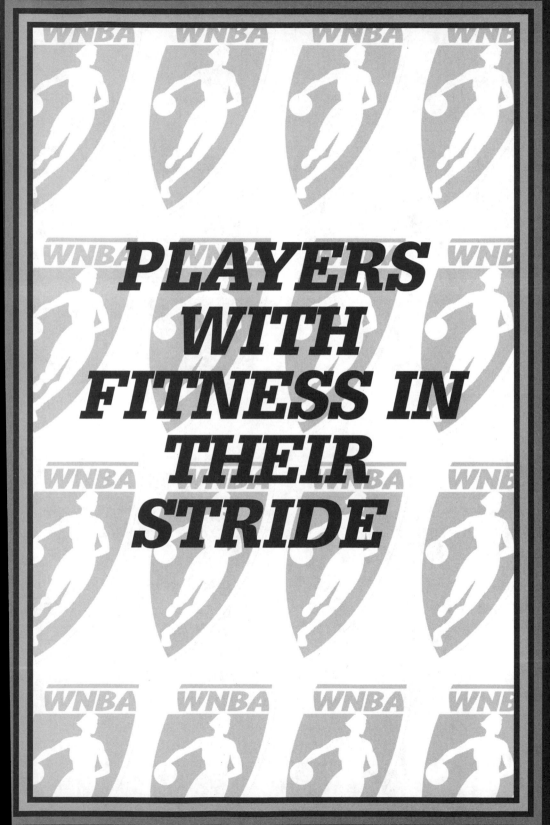

PLAYERS WITH FITNESS IN THEIR STRIDE

Nikki McCray

Nickname "Nik-Nik"

The basics:

> *team:* Washington Mystics
>
> *position:* Guard
>
> *height:* 5-11
>
> *weight:* 158 lbs.
>
> *date of birth:* 12/17/71
>
> *honors:* member of the gold medal-winning 2000 U.S. Olympic team, Mystics' leading scorer in 1998 and 1999, member of the gold medal-winning 1996 U.S. Olympic team

Typical workout in/off-season:

Whether Nikki is practicing with the Mystics or the National team, or just keeping in shape during the off-season, the number one important thing for her is to keep it fun. "Basketball isn't a job," Nikki says. "It's something I've enjoyed since I was little. And even when basketball is over, I'm always conditioning and running."

Other sports/activities she enjoys:

Hiking in the Tennessee mountains, water sports, watching soap operas and singing (Nikki has been known to chirp the national anthem at sporting events!).

What she eats:

Nikki says she eats a lot of carbohydrates and fiber to give her energy.

Fave "forbidden" treat:
French fries and McDonald's.

Thoughts about health and fitness:
"You can work out, you can run, you can lift all you want. But if you don't eat properly, that really plays a lot into your fitness and your performance out on the court."

Special honors:
In 2000, Nikki was named to the President's Council on Physical Fitness.

Words of wisdom for teens:
"It's got to be something you want to do. That's the number one thing. You can't let people pressure you into getting in shape."

Natalie Williams

The basics:

    team: Utah Starzz

    position: Forward

    height: 6-2

    weight: 217 lbs.

    date of birth: 11/30/70

    honors: member of the gold medal-winning 2000 U.S. Olympic team, first team all-WNBA 2000, selected as a Western Conference reserve in the 2000 WNBA All-Star game

Typical workout in/off-season:

Natalie says she works a lot harder in the off-season, lifting weights and trying to work on her individual game. She does a lot of yoga and deep-water conditioning programs, which she says really help strengthen her knees and prevent injury.

Other sports/activities she enjoys:

Reading, singing, volleyball (she was on the U.S. Women's Volleyball team at the 1991 and 1993 World University Games).

What she eats:

Natalie eats a lot of protein and carbs together, and tries to eat healthy, balanced meals — including lots of veggies, chicken, rice and milk. And she *always* has a bottle of water with her.

Get FIT! EAT Right! Be ACTIVE!

Thoughts about health and fitness:
"I think one of the most important things is to eat well. . . . My body belongs to me, and I know what I need. If I need vegetables, red meat, milk. . . . It's amazing how if you listen to your body how well it will talk to you."

What she did as a teen to stay fit:
Natalie played volleyball and softball, and ran track and field. In high school, she won a weightlifting contest, and was the Utah state long jump champion.

Words of wisdom for teens:
"Eat in moderation and stay active. Whatever you do — cheerleading, swimming, running after your boyfriend, anything — just stay active!"

Jennifer Gillom

Nickname "Jent"

The basics:

team: Phoenix Mercury

position: Center

height: 6-3

weight: 180 lbs.

date of birth: 6/13/64

honors: 1997-1999 Mercury's top scorer, All-WNBA first team 1998, member of 1988 gold medal-winning U.S. Women's Olympic team

Typical workout in/off season:

Jennifer likes to make exercise a part of her daily life. She has exercise equipment in her home and a basketball court in her backyard. And she loves walking her dog. At the end of the off-season, Jennifer usually hires a personal trainer to whip her into top shape. She says the motivation is great!

Other sports/activities she enjoys:

Tennis, listening to music, doing crossword puzzles.

What she eats:

Lots of protein and veggies for energy and nutrients. She's super big on stir-fry with lots of fresh vegetables.

Thoughts about health and fitness:

"When I work out, I'm in a better mood, and it's good for me mentally. It has improved my self-esteem and I feel confident in my appearance as well."

What she did as a teen to stay fit:
Jennifer played center field on her high school softball team, and also excelled at tennis and the high jump (no surprise there!).

Words of wisdom for teens:
"It's hard to motivate yourself to exercise, so round up your friends. You and the gang can head to the gym or the outdoor courts, go in-line skating in the park, or jump rope. It could even be as simple as taking a brisk walk after school."

CONCLUSION:
It's All in Your Head

Getting fit, eating right and being active are all separate components of total fitness. But they work together in very cool ways. There are so many aspects to a healthy body and mind — flexibility, endurance, strength, mental toughness, nutrition, motivation, dedication, enthusiasm — but it's not difficult to develop all of them, because one thing leads to another. Every component of a healthy lifestyle enhances another.

Once you begin to make fitness a priority, start thinking about eating three meals a day or join a yoga class, you'll start paying attention to other aspects of fitness and health. You'll find that they all help each other. Toning your muscles in the weight room might motivate you to take up swimming again. And with the energy you're burning in the pool, you may decide you need to eat three balanced meals a day. The more lifestyle adjustments you make, the easier it becomes to work fitness and health into your everyday life.

It's not just a physical response that causes this chain reaction where you're making more and more healthy choices. It's your mind that leads your body down the healthy path. As the women of the WNBA know, an active body develops a healthier attitude. When your body is healthy, it's easier to keep a positive outlook. And the best part is that there's no waiting — your outlook may brighten the very day you step foot in the locker room or hike up a hill! You're taking care of your body and getting fit and active — you rock!

Here's the thing: A positive attitude will motivate you and keep you active and engaged in life. It will give you the strength you need to realize that just because you let your healthy lifestyle slip for a few weeks does not mean that you're back at the beginning. Overall wellness is best accomplished when the changes are made slowly and integrated into your everyday life. You shouldn't force yourself to do exercises or eat foods that you hate. Fitness, health and activity should be incorporated into your lifestyle in easy, fun ways that make you proud of yourself.

You have all the basic tools you need to work toward total wellness. Be excited, committed and dedicated. But most of all, be kind to yourself. This body is yours alone, and it's your only one, so treat it with respect and kindness. Feed it well, but don't freak if you eat two helpings of chocolate cake. Get moving, but don't stress if you miss ski practice all week. Stay active, but don't worry about a lazy weekend on the couch watching TV. Those breaks don't mean you've had a fitness meltdown — you deserve a little R and R, too.

Total fitness is realizing that your mind and body will work well together if you give them the right tools, take care of them and listen to what they need. Have confidence and be proud of who you are and what you can accomplish. You're on your way to a healthy you — getting fit, eating right and being active.